D0700910

BOOKS BY LYALL WATSON

LIGHTNING BIRD

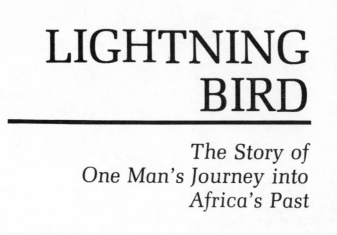

The Story of One Man's Journey into Africa's Past

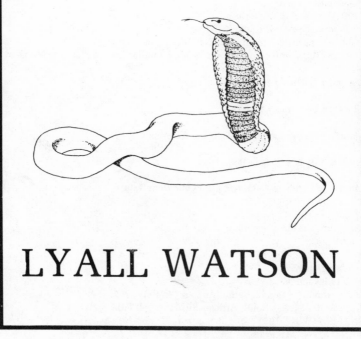

LYALL WATSON

A TOUCHSTONE BOOK
Published by Simon & Schuster, Inc.
NEW YORK

Copyright © 1982 by Lyall Watson
All rights reserved
including the right of reproduction
in whole or in part in any form
First Touchstone Edition, 1983
Published by Simon & Schuster, Inc.
Simon & Schuster Building
Rockefeller Center
1230 Avenue of the Americas
New York, New York 10020
Published by arrangement with E. P. Dutton, Inc.
TOUCHSTONE and colophon are registered trademarks of Simon & Schuster, Inc.

Designed by Nicola Mazzella

Drawings by Jacquey Visick

Manufactured in the United States of America

10 9 8 7 6 5 4 3 2   Pbk.

Library of Congress Cataloging in Publication Data

Watson, Lyall.
    Lightning bird.

    (A Touchstone book)
    Bibliography: p.
    Includes index.
    1. Boshier, Adrian. 2. Sotho (African people)
3. Anthropologists—South Africa—Biography. I. Title.
GN21.B594W37   1983   306'.092'4   83-13618
ISBN 0-671-47361-1 Pbk.

For
Raymond Arthur Dart—
the last of an epic breed.

There is a species of African bird that stands apart from all others.

Science knows it as *Scopus umbretta*, the hamerkop, and places it in a family of its own, midway between the storks and the herons. There is a little of each in its anatomy, but nothing of either in its behavior. It builds a nest-chamber about the size of a football and then encloses this in a superstructure big enough to fill an entire tree. Far too large to be accounted for in terms of survival value alone, this construction is more in the nature of a magnificent gesture, an act of deliberate defiance against the petty restrictions of natural selection.

People in Africa most often see the bird standing in pools of water, staring intently at its reflection. It is, they say, the one who knows the unknown; who is familiar with the things that vanish when you look directly at them. It is the one who stands alone; who cannot be pointed at; but who points out wizards and has access to their power. Pursued by the wind and the rain, this bird is known as a rainmaker, as a herald of the thunderstorm. It is—*mašianoke*—the Lightning Bird.

The people treat the hamerkop with elaborate respect, keeping their distance, but watching constantly for omens and portents in its behavior. Their regard is tinged with fear and colored by the belief that sometimes, perhaps once in many generations, the Lightning Bird takes it upon itself to appear among them in human form.

Contents

Foreword

This is the true story of Adrian Boshier, a young Englishman who arrived in Africa at the age of sixteen and ventured into the bush alone, on foot, equipped with nothing more than a pocket-knife and a plastic bagful of salt, to look for a world described a century earlier by Livingstone and Selous.

Against all the odds, he found it.

Sleeping in caves, living on bats and lizards, collecting and selling the venom from scorpions and snakes, he put himself through a punishing African apprenticeship. From the land itself he learned how to survive—what to eat and where to dig for water; the safe way to sleep and how to rob a lion of its prey; the art of keeping still and, most important of all, when to run prudently away.

For an Englishman to develop these skills was cause enough for renown. Few blacks and no whites of his generation could match his stamina and bushcraft, but for Boshier this prowess never became an end in itself; it was a way, with limited means, of staying out in the wild for as long and as often as he liked.

He lived like this for over twenty years, dipping into the wilderness at will, learning the ways of wildlife, exploring areas rich in fossils, cave paintings, stone tools, and ancient mines. At first the artifacts were objects of simple curiosity, but on one of his infrequent returns to civilization he met Professor Raymond Dart, doyen of African prehistory, who asked him difficult and relevant questions, told him what to read, and showed him what his findings meant.

Thus armed, Boshier returned to the wild and began to collect information in a more systematic way. Eventually he gathered material of sufficient worth to justify his appointment as Field Officer to the Museum of Man and Science in Johannesburg. Working from this base, he learned a great deal and soon became a peripheral but flamboyant presence on the local archaeological and anthropological scene.

For those, including myself, who met him during this period, he was an enigma. Tall, lean, and abrasive, he had a profound capacity to disturb. He had a hunter's nose, large and hyperactive. In the bush it flared in response to vanishing traces of musk or to a whisper of woodsmoke in the wind. But in the city, among people, he used it mercilessly, smelling out the bogus in any gathering, concealing his own latent unease in noisy exposure of the hypocrisy of others.

He was often cruel, highly intolerant of what he took to be signs of weakness in others, but he always reserved his harshest judgments for himself. He was a romantic, given to extravagant gestures and impossible ideals, destined to be disappointed in the world. He was frequently unhappy, but nobody who spent time with him was ever bored. He was a spellbinding raconteur, often difficult to believe, but impossible to ignore. Most academics considered him a dilettante and dismissed his stories as travellers' tales. It was easy to do so, because he published little and with great reluctance. But those who really listened to him, who bothered to look beyond the bombast, found there a lingering sense of rightness. You were left with the feeling that somehow this extraordinary character, without formal training or professional support, had succeeded on his own in reaching further into the true heart of Africa than any other explorer who ever lived.

Each time I met him, I struggled to find the key to Adrian Boshier. Part of the secret of his accomplishment lay in the fact that he walked everywhere he went. Few whites in Africa do. He was also widely respected by Africans for his willingness to eat whatever they ate and to drink their water. And a good part of Boshier's success must be attributed to his facility with snakes. He handled them fearlessly and well, and is still remembered with awe and reverence in many remote areas as Rradinoga, the "father of snakes."

These things were important, but all of them taken together fall short of explaining how he apparently managed to unlock some of Africa's best-kept tribal secrets. In 1978, at the age of thirty-nine, Adrian Boshier died—and I knew the answer. He had a secret of his own: he was severely epileptic.

The epilepsy that killed him also gave him access to the arcane. Throughout Africa, epileptic seizures are believed to be the result of possession by *badimo*, the spirits of the ancestors. Anyone who has such attacks is accorded special treatment, out of respect both to the victim and to the spirits who produce such a sacred disease. There is no cure for epilepsy, only treatments; and these Adrian Boshier refused to take. He fought a dreadful private battle against his spirits, crying out in alternate terror and derision in the midst of his convulsions. Recurrent attacks left him confused, nauseated, restless, and irritable, and these undoubtedly account for much of his complex personality. But they also left him with the respect of the people who saw similarities between his behavior, his spirits, and those of the tribal spirit-diviners. Like them, he was seen to have an African soul.

With knowledge of Boshier's secret, it was possible to understand how he had been admitted to the inner circles of tradition. It now became necessary to reevaluate everything he had said about what he had seen and done. Armed with and excited by this insight, I found it impossible to ignore a request from those closest to Adrian Boshier to try to pull his life and stories together into a comprehensible whole. This book is the result.

Adrian Boshier left a collection of tattered diaries and some notes toward the first draft of a book on his early experiences. I have tried to weave these, together with interviews with all those who knew him well, into a coherent form. To do this, I have had to rely on my memory of the stories as he told them; at times I have been forced to dramatize events for which no records exist. But the words are, I believe, true ones, in some cases taken from later interviews with the people involved.

The pattern of Adrian Boshier's life was extraordinary, but in a strange way it was almost preordained. It recreated, in miniature, all the crucial steps in our evolution, following the accepted sequence so precisely that I have chosen to punctuate the narrative with documentary asides that put what he did, and what I believe is the significance of his accomplishments, into proper perspective. I make no apology for taking liberties with time. The precise sequence of events in Boshier's short, hectic life is immaterial. This is not a biography. It is part homage to a powerful and unusual man and part scientific document, because I believe that what he did, what he found, and what we can learn from his experience, are of considerable value. For Boshier came closer than anyone I know to uncovering those intangible parts of old Africa that have become fossilized, not in the rocks, but in folklore and oral tradition. These pieces, I suggest, offer the best chance we have of unearthing what amounts to a prehistory of the mind. That is why I have chosen to deal with them at some length and why I see Adrian Boshier, the man who revealed them, as a figure of substance in African history, as a worthy inheritor of the power and tradition of the fabled Lightning Bird.

Boshier came nearer to opening this door to the prehistoric mind than even he knew, for his vantage point was unique. He went his own way, organized his own initiation, and saw magic when those around him were unaware that there was anything to see at all.

Africa owes him a debt. And as a child of the continent, I offer this book in part payment.

Dr. Lyall Watson.
"Marula," 1981.

Part One

*"The body may be broken,
as a cairn of stone is scattered;
but the spirit is there all the time."*

Sotho proverb.

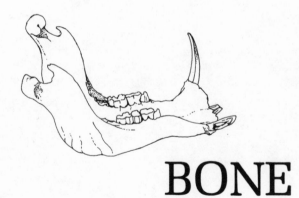

BONE

In Africa, as elsewhere, spirits abound. They exist on a plane that is higher than ours, but somewhat less than divine. And they are prone to a reassuring number of very human imperfections. Some spirits exercise a baleful influence over everyday affairs and need to be appeased by gifts and sacrifice. They have to be watched. But few people have the time or the experience necessary to keep constant vigil. Everyone, sooner or later, falls foul of a petulant shade.

Every community in Africa supports one or more specialists in dealing with such dilemmas. These dingaka are trained to act as spirit mediums, as go-betweens whose task it is to keep the peace, to maintain equilibrium between the visible and invisible worlds. They can do so directly, through contact made in trance or dream, but most diviners also use some sort of mechanical device.

The best known of these is a set of "bones." Each ngaka (singular of dingaka) has a unique personal collection of such

3

magical dice or ditaola, which may include the knuckle bones of totem animals, cowries, pieces of tortoiseshell, potsherds, and old coins. But at the heart of every set are four special tablets made of horn or wood or ivory. These are the "men" and "women," carved by craftsmen chosen for their skill and decorated, on one side only, with traditional motifs.

There is lekgolo—the centenarian, the Old Man, symbol of prosperity and strength;

kgadi—the Old Woman, who stands for motherhood and hospitality;

selume—the Youth, glowing with health and virility;

and lengwe—the Maiden, sign of pleasure and good fortune.

When new, the ditaola are all said to be "blind" or "unable to see the truth." They have to be broken in by an appropriate ritual, which often involves sprinkling them with an infusion of herbs mixed with the feces of a lark and leaving them overnight at a crossroads or other place of decision.

Then they are ready to "speak."

Questions are addressed to these "bones" by shaking them in the hands or in a small skin bag and throwing them out together into a pattern on the ground. The four main ditaola are marked on only one surface, so they can fall in sixteen different combinations. Each of these has a praise name, one traditionally given in its praise, and a meaning. Taken together, these symbolize all the stages of life and all the social roles of both sexes. If, for instance, all four pieces fall face upward, on their feet, they are said to be "walking" or "smiling," which is good. This pattern is known as likomeng, the whisper, the voice of those who know the secret songs.

Such a pattern helps to select one from a number of possible courses of action or answers, and gives this choice the blessing of tradition and ritual. It absolves those involved of direct responsibility by bringing them into tune with the wishes of the spirits. Like all methods of divination, the success of the "bones" depends largely on the person who reads them.

Likomeng—

"The secret songs"

In an old army hut with a tin roof on a university campus in Johannesburg, a magician presides over a room full of bones. Row upon row of mandibles, femurs, loose teeth, and horn cores lie on shelves and trestle tables, are neatly arranged in drawers, or overflow into wooden boxes on the floor. There are tens of thousands of skeletal fragments, all neatly numbered—the remains of more antelope, pig, and giraffe than anyone has seen together since the time of the great migrations.

The bones are surprisingly heavy. Each has lain so long beneath the earth that all its cells have been replaced by calcite or silica. Soil stuff has seeped into the tissue, keeping its precise shape, but taking its place, turning it into limestone. They are all fossils, rows of bone turned to stone by time.

The man responsible for this collection is an enthusiast, perhaps the last of an epic breed; he may be the sole survivor of a time of great scientific shamans. He is a small, balding, bouncy man who bubbles with conviction. His vitality is such that it seems to spill over onto the fossils and to jerk them back, like puppets, into life. As he moves among the bones, handling first one and then another, the fragments begin to bristle with design and purpose, becoming unquestionable cutters, scrapers, daggers, clubs, and probes. For this is no random assortment; it is a sampling from an ancient midden mound, the little that remains to tell us of the life and mind of early man.

Left to themselves, the bones are mute. But in the hands of a master they begin to sing. It takes a special sensitivity, a sort of scientific second sight, to bring out the best in them. Few have this talent, but those who do are able to coax the bones, not to augury, but into revelations about our past.

Raymond Dart is one of the few who read the bones very well. Adrian Boshier could not have had a better teacher.

There is a raw and elemental energy in Africa that does not seem to exist anywhere else in the world. It may have something to do with the fact that Africa is the birthplace of all humanity. For all humans, to go to Africa is to go home. What we find there is a message, but one that is difficult to read because the hominid fossils that decorate our family tree are still so scarce that there are more scientists than there are skulls for them to work on. Recent finds in Africa, however, are beginning to fill a few of the more glaring gaps, to give us some idea of our physical origins. The cradle of humanity seems to lie somewhere in South or East Africa, but who or what rocked it, and sent our ancestors scrambling up out of the Great Rift Valley, remains a mystery. We still know next to nothing about our psychic origins.

Our physical roots seem to lie on Africa's high plateaus, and every once in a long while one of them becomes exposed by wind, water, or the hands of a small band of dedicated fossil hunters. Paleontologists read volumes into every stray fragment, erecting elaborate deductive structures around isolated bones, giving us some idea of what our ancestors may have looked like and how they might have died. But none of these detectives of prehistory, no matter how skilled he or she may be in reconstructing ancient crimes, is able to tell us much about motives. We know nothing about how our earliest ancestors thought or felt, or what it was that lit the spark of consciousness.

There are still communities in Africa whose way of life has

changed little since the Late Stone Age. These delicate blooms cannot survive much longer and deserve careful study, but fortunately they are not alone. There are other, hardier, and more fundamental growths around them. Old Africa has an unnerving way of creeping up through cracks in even the most modern pavement. We are not going to learn from anyone now alive what it was like when our ancestors shared their nursery with the Australopithecines. But we do have much to learn from people whose lineage perhaps runs more directly than ours to the roots of "human-being"; and who embody, in their ways of seeing and in their systems of belief, a philosophy that is older than our own—and which may be closer to the truth.

Science today is a complex endeavor, in its method of discovery a little like the building of a railroad. It depends first on the explorers, the trailblazers who set out on their own into unknown territory, confident that there is somewhere to go. And it depends on engineers, those with the skill and patience necessary to follow the trail and turn it into a track that can be traveled even by those who take things as they come.

Our civilization runs on this ribbon. And it is kept running by armies of technicians who tinker constantly with the mechanism. They are familiar figures in our lives, these specialists with their badges and uniforms, making confident announcements about arrivals and departures. It is easy to assume that it is they who run the railroad. Until sooner or later, often with great reluctance, they are forced to admit delay, "due to circumstances beyond their control." It is then that we are reminded of the pioneers, of those who traveled alone and pointed out the way—the ones who knew the secret songs, who heard the whispers in the night.

The study of prehistory is a complex, expensive discipline practiced today by teams of specialists, including paleoanthropologists (who look for fossils), taphonomists (who investigate the way in which fossilization occurred), and experts in radiometrics (who date the finds). All are skilled in statistical techniques, knowledgable about computers, and adept at squeezing information out of abnormal distributions in apparently unrelated sets of figures. But even though the study of man has become virtually impossible without a computer, it was not always so.

The first hominid fossils to emerge from Africa were flung into the face of orthodoxy by a small group of scientific wild men, who were true pioneers. Of these, none has been more prolific, nor proved more seminal and prophetic, than Raymond Dart.

Dart came reluctantly to Africa in 1922 to take up a chair in anatomy at the new medical school of the University of the Witwatersrand. He was thrust into paleontology almost by accident, by the chance discovery of the fossilized skull of an infant which he called *Australopithecus africanus* and identified as hominid. This discovery has been described as one of the most significant finds ever made in the history of anthropology. The experts were skeptical, but half a century later we now have a number of such specimens from a wide area across the African plateau. Dart's baby is firmly established as one of a group of human precursors.

There are now sufficient quantitative data to feed the computers on which the new paleontology depends. The world of science is at last content that the Australopithecines existed, that they were social, bipedal, and probably used simple tools. The evidence is persuasive and the graphs most elegant, but they cannot in the end conceal the fact that all conclusions contained in them were anticipated half a century ago by a solitary enthusiast. In paleontology, as in divination, the success of the bones depends on the one who reads them.

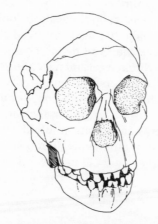

The particular strength and beauty of the Dartian approach, and its appeal to Adrian Boshier, is that it puts flesh on ancient bones. Dart's early men don't just die in convenient caves, they eat and think and bleed and wonder why. Dart turns fossils into beings and raises the whole difficult—and too often neglected—question of the role of mind in human evolution.

For those too remote from his collection to visit it in person, and for all those unfortunate enough never to have served, no matter how briefly, as apprentice to this magician—his conclusions remain difficult to accept.

One of the problems is that we have become used to defining man as a tool-using or tool-making animal, and concentrating all our attention on the material remains of early culture. We have become obsessed in particular with stone tools, perhaps because of their permanence and unquestionable status as human artifacts. And we have ignored nonmaterial, less permanent remains that might well have had more contemporary weight. In our haste to collect and classify the stones, we miss the simple things, the symbols, the evidence of behavior, and the possession and organization of knowledge.

Dart has long insisted that the division of early cultures into Early, Middle, and Late Stone Ages, solely on the basis of their stone implements, does not even have technical validity. It is merely an administrative convenience. It can also be grossly misleading, because it takes no account of the possibility, now clearly supported by studies of living people such as the San "Bushmen," that a large part of man's early equipment was probably made of perishable material such as hair, hide, grass, wood, and vegetable gourds.

We ought for this reason, he suggests, to look more carefully at those organic materials that have survived. This is precisely what Dart himself has done. And he has concluded that, before any of the recognized Stone Ages, man went through a formative Bone Age in which he developed an important culture. Dart calls this the *osteodontokeratic*, meaning bone-tooth-horn, culture.

There are still those who doubt that any such complex exists. They deny Dart's assertions of intelligence and foresight and prefer instead to explain the peculiar bone concentration as the result of scavenging by local carnivores or the differential resistance to weathering of various types of bone. Dart has tried to convince the doubters by playing their game, by accumulating sufficient evidence to prove his case by statistical significance. He insists that "there is nothing mystical about the way in which I get the bones to tell the story of the Australopithecine's hunting and dietary habits; rather it is a story of painstaking sorting and hammer-and-chisel work, combined with scientific deduction."

Part of his evidence is of this sort, but it is worth noting that all of his most far-reaching insights have come from an initial, almost intuitive, reading of the bones. Dart vehemently dismisses any suggestion that he may be psychic, but the fact remains that he is capable of exercising a very special sensitivity. He sees things in bones that are invisible and which remain contentious to his contemporaries—at least until they have the chance to work with him and learn to see things through his eyes; or until later finds prove, as they so often have, that his first impressions were right.

Dart was always certain, for instance, that jawbones containing a few teeth had been used as saws, and that bones twisted and broken into longitudinal slivers once served as simple knives. But there was no way he could prove either of these contentions until an unexpected helpmate, in the form of Adrian Boshier, arrived in June 1962.

"Professor," interrupted an assistant, "there's someone here you should talk to. He says he recognizes your bones."

Dart left his office to find Adrian Boshier waiting in the room full of bones. His first impression of the visitor was one of wildness, of something caught against its will in a hostile environment, like a stag at bay. The young man wore ordinary casual clothes, but he carried them with a certain reluctance, as though forced into uniform. The only things that seemed really to belong to him were the heavy, well-worn bush boots.

He was tall and thin, with the sort of rangy, angular build that sometimes conceals great strength. He was not a big man, but the size of his hands, the set of his jaw, and the thrust of his large nose all warned of a power not to be taken lightly.

Dart was amused by the aggressive stance of his young visitor, recognizing in it, and in the intensity behind the eyes, something of his own forthright, no-nonsense nature.

"What do you make of those?" he asked, indicating a case full of his bone "daggers."

"They're knives, of course," said Boshier positively.

"Why do you say that?"

"I know them well, Professor. Sharp bones exactly like these are still used for cutting the seeds out of marula fruit before the flesh is used for making wine."

"You mean they are still used today? Here in the Transvaal?"

"Oh yes. In fact I even have one."

Dart's eyebrows bobbed with excitement. "Where the devil can I get some?"

"Wherever the marula tree grows. I'll get them for you as soon as I return to the northern Transvaal."

Adrian Boshier explained that the *marula* or *morula* tree was so important to many Northern Sotho that theirs was almost a marula culture. The elegant, round-crowned trees, with their graceful compound leaves, were the only ones that were never cut when land was cleared for planting. One or more such sacred trees stand in every field, turning the otherwise bare plots into stately parkland. Everyone owned a marula tree, as everyone possessed a field. And only when all the trees in the fields and gardens had been denuded of their fruit, did the women pass on to those still growing in the bush far from the village.

"The golden fruits appear each year in February and March," he said, "when everything is green, when grass stands high, and weeding is the order of the day. Some of the fruit is eaten at this time. It has a pleasant sour-sweet taste. But people and animals alike prefer to wait a few days until the squashy golden carpet under the tree begins to ferment. It does so naturally, producing an alcoholic slush that leaves even elephants staggering. I have seen warthogs wandering off so drunk they can no longer raise their tails nor find their burrows.

"The people, however, have discovered how to make an even more potent brew. They gather each day of the marula season beneath the trees nearest their homes and collect the fruits as they fall, squeezing the juice into large clay pots. Fermentation starts immediately, producing a clear, sparkling, slightly aromatic drink that tastes a little like fruity champagne."

Dart was fascinated. "And what part," he asked, "do these knives play in the whole process?"

"A vital one," responded Boshier. "The marula was given to the people by the spirits and is therefore a 'big gift.' It has to be dealt with in the way of the ancestors. To drink the juice from it unfermented would be an insult, and a small portion from each brew is always set aside as an offering to the spirits. The initial cut into the ripe fruit is made with a special knife. Sometimes one of wood, but usually a blade made from the limb bone of a goat, sheep, or antelope which is split by blows from a sharp stone and polished smooth on a grinder. The spirits would be greatly offended if the people used a metal knife."

"Has it always been so?"

"As long as anyone can remember. The people eagerly look forward to the time of the marula. It provides a break from the usual chores and relief from drought and hunger. Most of the season is spent sitting out in the shade of the trees, preparing the brew right there on the spot and drinking prodigious quantities. There is a mighty hubbub in the bush, with an endless party under every tree. It is impossible for a stranger such as myself to walk through the country at this time without stopping off at every tree for a quick one. I sometimes become a little paranoid at the sight of the characteristic marula outline in the distance and try to make a wide detour, but there are so many trees that one cannot help bumping directly into another bunch of merrymakers. The whole bushveld is one extended party. By dark virtually everyone is thoroughly drunk and the night air is filled with discordant singing and drumming."

"But this is wonderful," Dart responded enthusiastically. "This is very important information. You are telling me something I didn't know, something that provides a vital link, a piece of cultural continuity that may extend back over a million years or more without change. And the fact that these people continue to use a bone tool, not a metal one, for an area in their lives that is considered most sacred, is highly significant. There is a direct association between the one sure way they have of transcending—of altering their consciousness, of reaching for oblivion, of forgetting their daily difficulties—and the survival of an ancient religious ritual with its special sacred tools."

This is vintage Dart. He never misses the chance to put behavior and symbology into perspective, to try to explain present human customs in terms of their historic and prehistoric past. He is particularly adept at picking out small things—the shape of a bone or a trace of pigment—and showing how they could have been part of a way of life, part of a simple pattern of community which became reshaped and transformed at a later period into another and more elaborate set of customs with new values.

It was also a revelation to the young visitor, who had never dreamed that it was possible to read so much into simple observations.

The following day Boshier returned to the Institute with his marula knife which, laid beside the fossil specimens, proved to be identical, crafted from similar tibial bones millions of years apart.

Dart was ecstatic. He even wept. "I have," he said, "little control over my sympathetic nervous system."

He turned his full attention to the young man who had walked into his life with this precious gift and demanded to know all about him—everything he had ever seen, heard, read, found, or believed in. Professor Dart made everything Boshier had done seem important and exciting. And the intense young man talked as he had never talked before. He told Dart of his childhood as an evacuee from war-torn England to the United States, and of his return to Europe in 1946 when he was sent to one of the first "outward bound" schools, in which he was encouraged to be self-sufficient, to look after himself. He spoke of his early and abiding passion for the Old Africa as glimpsed in the books of Stanley, Livingstone, Burton, and Selous; and of his dreams of following in their footsteps. He had devoured everything he could find written on African wildlife, but the dream seemed an impossible one for anybody in postwar Europe, let alone one without even graduation qualifications. Then the miracle had taken place. His mother married a man who was about to take up a teaching position in South Africa and the whole family had emigrated in 1955.

Boshier explained how, just a few days after their arrival in Johannesburg, unable to contain his impatience any longer, he had hitchhiked out of the city carrying nothing but his treasured pocketknife and a bag of salt which, he knew from Stanley's accounts, was likely to prove useful for trading. As the cars carried him away from civilization, he had, in his innocence, kept asking the drivers, "Is this the bush? Have we arrived yet?" And when one, finally tiring of the incessant question, had said, "Yes, this is it," he had simply got out and walked away, directly into the past.

Dart was deeply impressed by the initiative of this young man who had, on his own, without training or any previous experience, just walked into the wild and learned how to survive there; who had indeed spent most of the six years since his arrival in Africa, living alone in the bush. By the time that night fell and everyone else had left the Institute, the two of them were still in deep conversation. Dart learned, among other things, of Boshier's fascination with snakes, of his compulsion for catching them, and of how news of this strange behavior had spread rapidly through the land. The African people were also impressed that he, a white man, should be walking everywhere without car or equipment. Unable to accept that this should be so, the village chiefs would keep sending out runners to backtrack him and find out where he had hidden his vehicle.

As he talked, Boshier began to realize, for the first time in years of solitary and often aimless exploration, that, despite his lack of formal education, he might have something to offer the academic world. At the end of their meeting, the professor made Adrian Boshier the offer of his life. He promised to show him what to read and to tell him what it meant, and to squeeze a small financial grant out of a charitable trust—on the condition that Boshier used it to continue his sorties into the bush, returning from time to time to report.

Boshier was overwhelmed and, with uncharacteristic diffidence, expressed surprise that Dart should even consider taking on someone without any qualifications at all. Dart's eyes flashed and his brow wrinkled in indignation. "How many bloody people do you think are receiving an education like yours? Universities all over the world are turning out thousands of graduates each year, but the African wilderness trains very few. Now you get back out there as fast as you can. And no damn nonsense about cars or fancy equipment. You go the way you have always gone. On foot."

And Adrian Boshier went.

Part Two

*"The lizard that lives on the rocks,
still carries the dust of long ago."*

Sotho proverb.

STONE

Africa was our cradle. We were born in its central highlands something like five million years ago. The record of our childhood still lies there, embedded in the bony breccia of limestone caverns, or disinterred and scattered across the dry floor of the Great Rift Valley.

Our ancestors were probably never very numerous. We have scarcely enough of them, taken altogether, to fill even a small church hall. But it seems that this was sufficient—a quorum as it were—the right number necessary to take the first vital steps. For a million years ago all of Africa, as well as the nearer parts of Europe and Asia, were peopled by another breed, a new human generation. Brash in the manner of all adolescents, but vigorous and inventive, they glowed with the first sparks of true creativity.

The process began with the southern man-apes, the Dartians, whose liberated hands were the first to reach for tools. The question of their culture remains moot, but it is certain that they used those simple aids, extensions of their own arms, which came most easily to hand: long bones with clublike ends, horns with the points of daggers, and mandibles with teeth large enough to cut or rip. It is inconceivable that these were not used, often, and with increasing skill.

The first time may have been accidental. And the second. But sooner or later in each small community of foragers, there would have been an individual more inventive than the others, someone able to see the potential in these ready-made aids. Such a being would be able to make the conceptual leap necessary to pick one up deliberately and bend it to some chosen end. This was a big thing, a giant step in human evolution, but in a very real sense it was almost inevitable.

In every society, even those of living apes and monkeys, there are gifted individuals who exploit their environments to the full, exploring all possibilities. And each conspicuous success, especially if it offers some advantage, soon becomes imitated by others.

Such individual variation among our early ancestors undoubtedly lay behind the leap from tool-using to simple tool-making; from recognition of the useful qualities in a sharp bone, to an attempt to reproduce this desirable quality in another bone. The result was the individual invention of new tools to suit new needs.

We know from the number of bruised pebbles found in association with our ancestors that it was not long before handy rocks were added to the natural armory of bone, tooth, and horn. Hammer stones came first and then simple choppers, made by knocking off a couple of flakes to provide a sharper edge. These tools are so crude that there are still those who refuse to accept them as artifacts. They become significant only by virtue of their number and their persistent association with the bones of early hominids.

It is possible to argue about the degree of industry and humanity of the makers, but there is no question about their successors. Starting about a million years ago, all caves, campsites, and living floors became littered with objects that were unquestionably tools. These were classic hand axes, extraordinary almond- or tear-drop shaped objects, chipped with care on both sides into elegant symmetrical forms.

The first such hand axes to be described came from St. Acheul in the Somme Valley. The French called them bouchers or coups de poing, but they are known everywhere else as Acheulian hand axes. And an astonishing fact is that they are found everywhere else that early man occurred. They were the Boy Scout knives of the ancient world.

European hand axes are made of flint, some Middle Eastern ones of chert, and those in Africa of quartzite, diabase, or indurated shale. But wherever they have been found, they are remarkably similar. There is an unmistakable unity of style and design that cannot be explained by the parallel and independent evolution of similar answers to the same human needs. There is nothing logical about a hand ax; its shape bears no relation to the form in which rocks are found or will fracture. It is totally irrelevant in terms of natural suggestion; that is, it could never have arisen as a result of simple trial and error. It was certainly popular enough, but it is difficult to imagine how it could ever have been used.

Wherever prehistorians meet, wild and entertaining guesses are made, but we have no evidence to support any of the conjectures. No function we can imagine seems to demand that specific shape, which clearly required a massive investment of skill and care.

The most mysterious and wonderful thing about the hand ax is that it is unnecessarily beautiful. The delicacy and symmetry in its design, the quality of the workmanship involved, and the time devoted to its manufacture, all go far beyond functional demand. Why did they go to all this trouble? Why did they bother, when a cruder instrument, much more simply made, would have been just as effective?

There is no obvious solution to the presence of this same lovely artifact across so wide an area, nor to its persistence over so long a period of time. But there is no question about its importance or its significance; it was our first specialized, inarguable tool. It ushered in the Stone Age and it laid the foundations for both technology and art. It was our first essay in style, the first real evidence of creativity.

Stone is a much more demanding medium than bone. It offers a far more rigorous exercise in creative thinking. A bone has a natural form that is suggestive of possible function, but most rocks are irregular and intractable. Sculptors of stone must make formidable mental leaps. They have to be able to imagine the shape in the stone and find some way of releasing this imprisoned form. Our ancestors did this, successfully, and in the process became truly human.

Morutiwa—

"The apprentice"

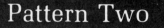

After having been half drowned by a flash flood that brought a dry riverbed back to turbulent life in the night, and after being almost blinded by a squirt of venom from the thick tail of a scorpion that tried to share his blanket, Adrian Boshier had learned to choose his campsites with great care. He had discovered that some places were appealing, while others, for no apparent reason, were almost repugnant. The distinction between the two was clear. It seemed to have nothing to do with his own preference, or to be associated in any way with particular landscapes, trees, rocks, hilltops, clearings, or caves.

Boshier learned to recognize the right "feeling" and, if necessary, to continue walking until well after nightfall, secure in the knowledge that when the place was "right," he would know. He would then be able to unroll his blanket with a sense of well-being, even in total darkness. He had found that it is not necessarily what you like, but what likes you, that matters.

So he always traveled until he found such a place of accep-

tance, where he stopped. And there he slept, lying fully extended on his stomach, never once moving. He had trained
himself to do this in order to minimize the danger of rolling over
onto anything that might be attracted to his warmth in the night.
It had happened more than once that he had found a lethal puff
adder coiled up alongside him at dawn and, because he slept
quietly and woke without thrashing about, no harm had come to
either of them.

On one memorable morning, soon after his first meeting
with Raymond Dart, he awoke to find himself beneath a wild fig
tree. As the first light touched the upper branches, burnishing
the leaves, a flight of turacos swept in on crimson wings. Dark
tails fanned on landing, purple crests erect, they disappeared
into the foliage, jumping rather than flying from branch to
branch. One leaned over to peer at him, head cocked to show a
bright red eye, while the others set about the figs, gossiping
among themselves with long, contented, rounded sounds.

He thought about breakfast. The wild figs, though edible, were
not very exciting. There were times when he had lived on them,
joining black-faced vervet monkeys up in the canopy, selecting
the softer fruits that grew directly from the branched gray trunks.
But every single fig was crawling with incidental life—alive
with minute worms, almost too small to see unless you happened to be looking for them. These were the larvae of tiny
parasitic wasps that pollinated the flowers, or the little white
maggots of a host of African fruit flies. They too were edible,
even nourishing, but it took an effort of will to swallow them.

Some worms were actually very good. Boshier had discovered this when coming once upon a band of people apparently picking fruit from a grove of mopane, trees with large
double leaves that droop like the wings of resting butterflies.
Mopane grow in hot, low-lying lands and in midsummer each
year are host to myriads of emperor moths, some of the largest in
the world, with heavily scaled wings, each bearing a conspicuous eye-spot that makes them look like disembodied owls. The
females lay their eggs on the tree and a few weeks later the larvae
emerge and gobble their way, like cannibals, through the butter-
fly leaves. Very soon they grow into plump, hairless caterpillars
about three inches long with bodies handsomely banded in

yellow, white, and red. And very soon, a host of people descend on the groves like locusts and collect every caterpillar in sight.

Boshier joined in the excitement and before long someone offered him a handful of lightly roasted worms. He had accepted them with some uncertainty, but never liking to offend, had put at least one into his mouth. The initial sensation of the insect's spiky legs was most unpleasant, so he had quickly crunched the whole thing up and swallowed it. To his surprise, he found that it did not taste at all bad, and soon he was eating them as voraciously as the people. After a day or two he became so accustomed to the whole thing that he was quite unconcerned by the look or feel of the caterpillars and came to enjoy their savory flavor equally well whether grilled or raw.

Boshier's need to know how to live off the land grew out of an early humiliation. While walking a forest path one day, he glimpsed in the distance figures moving swiftly away through the trees. New to Africa, he did not stop to think that he might be the cause of their flight. He continued on his way until he came to the spot where he had seen the fleeing forms. And there, right in the middle of the path, lay a large, ripe papaya. At first he thought the figures must have dropped it in their haste, but soon realized that if they had, it would have burst.

Unsure of their motives, but certain of his hunger, he sat down and ate the entire fruit. He went on down the trail wondering why, if their gesture had been one of goodwill, his benefactors had fled. A few hundred yards further, four fowl eggs lay neatly arranged at his feet. There was no doubt that these had been deliberately left for him, so he consumed them as well.

He never did discover who the people were or why they had been so generous. It never happened again and he was later able to dismiss the whole incident as one of the many inexplicable but intriguing things that happen in Africa when one steps off the beaten track. But at the time it disturbed him a great deal. The gift was welcome and the food was good, but he was humiliated by the fact that he needed this kind of assistance, and that his need was apparently so obvious to others. This was not what he had had in mind when he had set out to live off the land. So he had determined, from that moment on, to relearn all the ancient skills of hunting and gathering, to put himself in the position of being able to offer surplus food rather than having to receive it.

It had not been easy. One of the first lessons he learned had been in scavenging.

Boshier was trudging along in the heavy sand of a dry riverbed when the "whoosh" of a passing bird, traveling fast, made him look up. Winging down the watercourse went a peregrine falcon, eyes bright, intent on prey beside a pool at the bend. As it swooped down at the water's edge, there was a flurry of smaller birds, exploding out and away from the spot in panic. Then, before this commotion subsided, it was brought to a new crescendo by a series of bloodcurdling screams.

A black figure leaped out of the reeds beside the pool and came running toward him, flinging missiles into the air. It looked as though he was under attack by hostile tribesmen. He turned to run, but stopped when he realized that the maniacal howl had changed to laughter as his attacker came to a halt and was joined by several other black and equally merry friends who materialized out of the reeds.

The men ran together across the sand to retrieve the body of a turtledove dropped by the startled falcon. They were unarmed except for a bunch of throwing sticks, and invited him to join them in their hiding place. There they sat until peace was restored and flocks of small birds returned to the pool to drink.

The next victim was a red-necked falcon, drawn to the pool by the chance of easy prey, but the result was the same: the men erupted from the reeds, yelling and throwing their sticks into the air. The raptor shied in alarm, opened its talons, wheeled away in confusion, and another body was added to the growing pile of stolen prey.

From that day on Boshier used the technique himself, producing a state something like paranoia among the local birds of prey.

Later he went on to bigger things. He became a hunter, taking fledglings from their nests, lassoing lizards, spearing fish, and running down and strangling young antelope with his bare hands.

One hungry week he headed for a valley where *dassie*—small, brown, rabbitlike rock hyraxes—were common. It was a deep, narrow gorge with sheer walls broken by irregular ledges. As he entered, the little mammals set up a whistling chorus of alarm calls and darted into their dens. He fixed his attention on a fat young one and noted exactly where it had disappeared. He then hurried up to the spot and, climbing onto a ledge above the hole, lay there with his knife lashed to a pole, waiting for it to reappear. An hour later, a few of the hyraxes had returned to sun themselves on the rocks, but his intended victim remained with no more than a cautious nose stuck out of its crevice. Just when it seemed about to emerge, there was a renewed chorus of alarm and all the animals disappeared again. He looked up in time to see the spotted breast of a giant martial eagle, quartering the broken slopes.

He was stiff and disgusted and about to leave when a small antelope, a klipspringer, appeared on the far side of the valley. The little animal came bounding along the ledges with all the alpine assurance of its species, stopping occasionally with all four hooftips perched on a minute foothold. Boshier watched its progress, wishing that it were on his side of the ravine.

Suddenly there was a blur as something feline fell through the air. It took him a few moments, the klipspringer's last, to realize that he had just seen a leopard pouncing on its prey. The cat held onto the antelope's throat until all reflex movement ceased. Then, pausing to look around, it swung the buck up as though it weighed no more than a rag doll, and went up the sheer rock face with all the ease and grace of a house cat jumping onto a windowsill. And when it reached the top of the valley wall, it disappeared into the thick bush.

Boshier crossed the ravine as quickly as possible and pulled himself cautiously up over the other rim. There was so much commotion going on in the bush that he thought there must be two leopards involved in a dispute. Nevertheless, he crawled into the thicket and lay there watching an astonishing scene.

The leopard took the hind leg of the antelope between its teeth and swung the corpse around so vigorously that it crashed through a thicket of thorn. Then, changing grip to its foreleg, the leopard repeated the whole procedure. Boshier wondered if it might be playing with its food, as cats will, but it soon became clear that there was nothing playful about the behavior. It was an intense and deliberate maneuver.

One of the most peculiar things about the klipspringer is its thick, rough coat. Each hair is hollow and spiky, like a short and brittle porcupine quill. These are sharp and uncomfortable to the touch. But if one grasps a handful of bristles, even on a live animal, they come away quite easily, leaving a bare patch on the skin. The leopard seemed to know this, because it was raking its prey through the thorny undergrowth until the whole thicket was covered in loose spiny hair and the antelope was almost bald.

When the leopard showed signs of settling down to feed, the watcher let out a stream of yells and began to thrash around him with his makeshift spear. The cat leaped to its feet and bolted.

Boshier paused only long enough to cut the hindquarters away and then went back down into the valley, leaving the rest of the meal to the carnivore that had killed it.

Over the years he became quite adept at depriving predators of their prey. But one day, inevitably, he met his match. Five lions had just pulled down a fully grown zebra and Boshier coveted at least a small part of their kill. The scare technique had worked before with two lions, so he decided that approximately twice as much commotion should be effective with five. He scooped up a couple of rocks and a piece of wood and rushed headlong into the clearing, trying to give the impression that he was a whole crowd of hungry people.

He bellowed. One of the lionesses lifted her head, stared at him impassively; and went back to her meal. He yelled louder and hurled one of the rocks. All five heads came up and looked at him with mild distaste. He was appalled at their indifference and faltered slightly, but it was too late to stop. He couldn't turn his back on the pride. He screamed until his throat hurt, and eventually one of the great cats got up and moved away.

It was a strange—and slightly foolish—situation to be in. Here he was, out in the open, bawling at a group of lions who didn't seem to give a damn!

The departure of one gave him a little confidence, however, so he flung himself about, still yelling wildly. Three more of the big cats retired to a safe distance, but the remaining lion, a large black-maned male, still firmly held his ground. Then sheer terror took over and Boshier behaved like a maniac, rushing forward and hurling his missiles. All the lion did was growl and shift a little to the side. Boshier shifted too, to the opposite side, and still screaming and dancing, made a dash for the nearest tree. Twenty feet up in a matter of seconds, gagging with fear and drenched with cold sweat, he looked back across the clearing.

The lion had not moved. It gave one long last disdainful look and returned to its interrupted meal.

Unrestrained behavior of this order is rare, or even certifiable, in our society, but there may have been a time when such antics had survival value. We have been hunters for nearly a million years, and our ancestors lived in much the same way for two or three million years before that. The biology of our species was created largely during this period, when we learned to become practicing, habitual carnivores. This is the only way in which we conspicuously differ from all other primates and it is difficult not to conclude, with Robert Ardrey, that "man is man, and not a chimpanzee, because for millions upon millions of years we killed for a living." It is therefore of considerable interest to find out, if we can, how the transition from vegetarian to carnivore came about.

One possibility is that, before we learned to hunt successfully in large, well-armed bands, we might have begun to enjoy the taste and the benefits of big game animals by stealing them from other predators. In his early days in the bush, this is precisely what Adrian Boshier was forced to do. He had to scavenge.

We know now that several primates, particularly baboons and chimpanzees, when they can, will kill and eat small antelopes and birds. But, as far as we can tell, none of them will ever eat meat killed by another species. Unlike humans, they show absolutely no interest in carrion.

There are, however, groups of living human hunters who have become highly specialized scavengers. The Hadza of Tanzania, who build their camps high up on the rocks overlooking the plains around Lake Eyasi, have become very skilled at interpreting the movements of vultures overhead. When the ever-present umbrella of vultures breaks and begins to spiral down in a more purposeful way, they follow the birds and track down fresh kills even many miles away. They drive wild dogs, leopard, and lion off a carcass without any hesitation by rushing in on the carnivores with wild yells and gesticulations. Admittedly, they possess powerful bows and arrows and it is likely that the predators have learned to respect these and keep a safe distance.

Poorly armed early man may have had more trouble. There have been several attempts by anthropologists to demonstrate that it is possible for men on foot, without weapons, to put leopard and lion to flight; but these have all been experiments in parks or other areas in which the animals have become used to, and have acquired some fear of, human activity. And there were usually others with rifles sitting in a vehicle a short distance away in case anything went wrong.

What Adrian Boshier demonstrated is that it is possible for a single human, on foot, alone, unarmed, and a long way from others of his kind, to succeed in stealing food from a big cat . . . and that it is equally possible for him to fail, with possibly fatal consequence.

Scavenging may have been useful, but it could never have been reliable enough to bring about a major evolutionary change in our forebears. The dangers of wild animals have certainly been exaggerated, particularly by white hunters, but Boshier's experience, and the evidence we have from the lives of full-time hunters and gatherers, suggests that hunting small, easily captured prey is far simpler and more nearly universal than scavenging. We also learn that scavenging carcasses from the larger predators, particularly those that have not been trained to stay away from man, can be difficult and dangerous.

There is new evidence to show that butchering sites—places where elephants and extinct dinotheres were trapped and cut up with the aid of crude stone tools—existed in Africa as long as two million years ago, long before the full development of the modern human brain.

It seems that man became a hunter very early on and, being the perfect opportunist, also scavenged whenever he could get away with it. But it is important to appreciate that he could have scavenged successfully only once he became so dangerous, so well armed, that he was able to drive the larger carnivores off their kills with impunity.

In the beginning, opportunism was the key to survival. Evolving man must have satisfied his hunger with whatever he could find, catch, or digest. When fruits ripened, he ate them, worms and all. When caterpillars swarmed, he joined in the scramble for protein. And when meat could be caught, trapped, strangled, or stolen without undue risk, that too is what he must have done.

Adrian Boshier learned these lessons, but first he had to unlearn and discard a whole complex of inhibitions and taboos acquired as a result of growing up in a society of specialists who hunt, kill, clean, grow, find, and transport food for the rest of the population. Only then was Boshier free to start again.

Fortunately he was young and strong and in the first few years following his arrival in Africa, without any prompting and in his own small way, he recapitulated three million years of human evolution—accepting vegetarian "handouts," foraging for himself, hunting as he learned the necessary techniques, and stealing prey from predators when he had acquired sufficient bravado.

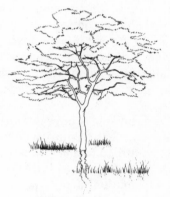

The turacos left the fig tree and flew down into the valley toward the river. Boshier followed. The open parkland gradually gave way to denser stands of fever trees with their powdery yellow bark. Overhead the fine foliage was alive with the static of colonies of masked and spotted-backed weavers, while under-foot the ground cover became thicker, forcing him where there was no trail to push through clumps of grass and sedge with his stick. Suddenly he broke out into a clearing of hard red soil. And, as suddenly, he saw his breakfast. A long, slender, green snake was gliding over the open ground toward cover on the far side. It was a boomslang, one of Africa's most abundant tree snakes.

These are essentially arboreal; among the branches they are

wonderfully agile, gliding silently through the greenery, moving with grace and speed, supporting themselves with acrobatic precision on two or three strategic twigs. But on the ground they are somewhat clumsy; on the rare occasions that they do descend, they are usually easily caught. As a rule, tree snakes make every effort to escape when disturbed. When cornered, however, they put on a great show, inflating their necks to twice the normal size and exposing patches of vivid dark skin between the scales. This one felt cornered and, to Boshier's surprise, not only blew out its throat, but actually attacked.

Its fangs are small and placed so far back that it is difficult for a tree snake to make a clean bite on anything as large as a human. But the venom glands, small as they are, contain one of the most potent of all known hemotoxins. It was one for which there was then no antidote, so Boshier decided at first to exercise discretion and retire.

When he realized, however, how thick the undergrowth was, instead of battling through territory where the snake would have the advantage, he turned to meet it, lunging at it with his stick. To his further surprise, it then turned and fled, as such snakes are supposed to do. Confident now that it was after all a normal boomslang, he went after it again, trying to get a grip on its retreating tail.

At the far end of the clearing, the tables were turned yet again as the snake reared up once more in a hissing attack, sending him back to his corner. And so the extraordinary battle raged, to and fro, as he and the snake took turns in chasing each other around the forest floor. Finally they stood face to face in the center of the arena, making alternate lunges until, with a lucky stroke, he managed to force its head down and pin it with his stick. It was then a comparatively simple matter to hold the writhing body against a tree trunk and sever the head with his knife.

This strange encounter was the first of many that Boshier was to have with snakes, but he was not to find many that would carry through an attack with such persistence. Boshier felt triumphant and hungry and decided to roast the snake right there over a fire made with a few dry and aromatic branches from the surrounding fever trees.

He skinned the reptile with a deft slit and a rip and had just got the fire going when he noticed a movement beside a tree just beyond the clearing.

He looked again, more carefully, and was astounded to see a man sitting there on the ground with his back against the trunk of a tree. He had obviously been there throughout the encounter. Adrian Boshier knew that this would be talked about and that it would not necessarily do his reputation any harm. But what he did not realize, until much later, was that in addition to his apprenticeship to the bush, he had, almost by accident, taken precisely those steps which are seen to be essential preparations for the most select of all African initiations.

Peetla—

"The rise of the cobra"

There is in African custom an essential harmony, an equilibrium with the land which seems to be lacking in our lives.

The people show this most clearly in the strength and propriety of their beliefs about, and their understanding of, the natural world. Many even identify themselves with a particular plant or animal, believing that there is a group spirit or soul, a collective identity that is equated in some way with this totem.

Each clan has its siboko, around which it is united, and which distinguishes it from all other clans. The attributes of the totem become those of the clan and may be embodied in its ritual. "What do you dance?" the villagers asked when Boshier became a part of their lives. At first he did not understand, but later learned that this is always what people in Africa say when they want to know the origins of a stranger.

The reply, "I dance the owl," for instance, means that the visitor comes from a community that recognizes the owl as its totem and is related not only to the bird, but historically to all other clans which know the same siboko.

There is an implicit connection between the name of a thing and the thing itself. A man and his name are often regarded as identical. And a personal or tribal name is a thing of power and significance, not to be given away lightly. It is a person's spirit.

The totem is also a thing of the spirit, and so a man and his name and his spirit and his totem are all one. And (arguing on the basis that things that are equal to the same thing are equal to one another) if a man and a bird are called by the same name, they must belong to the same species.

A natural consequence of this belief is that the totem becomes taboo for the clan. Boshier learned that the killing of an owl by a man called "Owl" is regarded as equivalent to the murder of a clan member, and is treated as such.

No member of a clan will eat his totem animal, nor sit near a member of another clan who may be handling its feathers or skin. The porcupine people told him, "It is taboo for us even to tread on the dung of noko, lest our feet break out in boils."

At a purely superficial level, such taboos seem nothing more than silly superstitions; but there is little doubt that they play a vital role in African society and must have considerable survival value. One possible function lies in the way totems can help to enforce an incest taboo. It is normally forbidden for people of the same clan to marry. In complex communities it may be difficult for even the keepers of tradition to remember all genealogies and to ensure that relatives do not interbreed. For such communities, the totem system provides a convenient shorthand for identifying those who share a bloodline.

Originally, each chiefdom had its own totem. Among the Sotho, for instance, the Ngwaketse chose kwena, the crocodile; the Tawana venerate phuti, the duiker; the Malete are identified with nare, the buffalo; the Tlokwa with thakadu, the aardvark; and the Kgatla with kgabo, the baboon.

When a group broke away from its original locale, it retained its original totem so that it is possible even today, when chiefdoms are confused by constant intermingling, to determine affinities by simply asking, "O binang? What do you dance?"

It is also possible that totemism provides a simple and effective form of conservation. If each clan regards certain species as taboo, this guarantees that those plants or animals will have an area in which they are protected and can multiply—or, at the very least, that predation on them in an area of mixed clans will be partially controlled. Each people, however, chooses a limited number of species as its totems. And these include not only those they find most useful or edible, but also ones identified as merely interesting or even dangerous.

The origins of totemic belief are clearly mixed, but it seems likely that one of its most important functions, in biological terms, is that it helps develop an affinity between a people and their habitat. It emphasizes similarity with nature and encourages a sense of that reverence for life that is fundamental to good ecology.

In the final analysis, it may well be impossible for any conscious creature, caught between the rival demands of body and mind, to live in seamless organic unity with the universe. The existence of totemism, and the emphasis on ritual, are both timely reminders that even tribal people lack complete spontaneity and have to reconcile their needs and their beliefs by leading carefully structured lives.

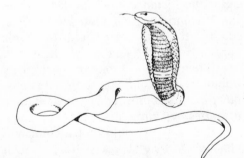

Adrian Boshier was beginning to appreciate this even before he discovered that he had a totem of his own.

A few days after arriving in Africa, he walked onto a Johannesburg golf course, and in a patch of bush beside the tenth fairway, had his first encounter with his totem.

He was halfway through a step when he saw the huge pile of scaly coils. With one foot still in midair, he froze, but the snake was less inhibited. It rose up to face him with its hood expanded to display a glossy black throat crossed by bands of vivid white. With a shock of recognition, based on a book about African reptiles, he realized that he was face to face with a *rinkals*, the continent's most accomplished spitting cobra.

This snake is renowned for its irritability, rearing up at the least provocation to show most of its four or five feet of dark, heavily scaled body. Its fangs are comparatively short and it seldom actually bites with deliberation, but it has large muscular poison glands which squirt the venom under pressure down the fang canals.

The poison ducts open, not on the tip of the fang as with most other snakes, but on the leading edge, so that two thin streams of toxin are forced out into the air, where they atomize into a fine spray. This travels many feet and is directed with uncanny accuracy at an enemy's eyes. The effect is instantaneous and devastating. The eye tissues are rapidly and painfully destroyed, producing complete blindness unless they are rinsed within seconds with oil, milk, or some other bland solution.

Boshier inched away to a safe distance and sat down to ponder the situation, and to stop his knees knocking together. Now was his chance to prove himself by catching a truly lethal snake. He decided to find a suitable stick. Crossing the fairway he realized that he was still walking on tiptoe, which looked both silly and suspicious, but he was finding it hard to control himself. He located a useful stick, trimmed it into the classic shape, and began the dreaded return.

Part of him wanted to get away and leave the dangerous animal to its own devices, but something even stronger willed him to return. He hoped desperately that the snake would by now have disappeared, but when he got back to the spot, it was still there, lying now full length on the ground.

He stood for a while and watched, taking great breaths of air.

Then, with an enormous effort, he forced himself forward and stood with his stick poised, wondering whether he was going to be strong enough to keep it pinned down. Finally he lunged.

As the stick closed over its neck, the snake erupted into a thrashing tangle of coils. It lashed out with its body and, to Boshier's dismay, managed to anchor its tail about his knee. He found small comfort in the thought that it was not a constrictor. It continued to hiss and writhe and whip the air while he hung on desperately, clinging to the stick with both hands.

Eventually the snake began to tire. Its lashings became more and more feeble until it lay, at last, quite still. But the battle was not yet over. Boshier still had to grasp the snake itself.

"I have never again had to exert such will and nerve," he said later. "Bending down and grasping that snake behind the head, was the most difficult thing I have ever had to do."

It left him trembling and exhausted, but he succeeded in carrying the snake all the way back to his new home and securing it there in a pillowcase. Then he was violently ill.

There could have been no better introduction to Africa, a continent in whose myth and lore snakes play a dominant role.

In the beginning, so the story goes, there was the Great Serpent, the first being, whose seven thousand coils set the planet and the stars in motion. This cosmic snake brought life to the earth by gouging out channels for rivers and streams. He can still be seen, moving in the current of a river, or lashing up the waves of the sea.

He is the divine python, arching in the form of the rainbow and flashing in the lightning. He lives in a cave deep underground, from which he will finally emerge to destroy his creation.

The ability of all snakes to shed their skin and reappear in a new body at regular intervals, has led to a widespread belief in their immortality. The symbol of eternity in African lore is a coiled snake with its own tail in its mouth. Snakes are imbued with supernatural powers of wisdom and the secret of eternal youth. They represent the forces of life and regeneration, exercising a profound influence over fertility and good fortune. Of course, since they also deal out death, snakes are held in awe in Africa and throughout the world. They have become objects of both fear and respect, veneration and revulsion.

In Africa, snakes are regarded as reincarnations of the spirits of the ancestors. Homage is paid to them in the form of images—either naturalistic or simply in the form of wavy lines molded into rings, carved on masks, printed on cloths, or painted on the walls of houses. Snakes are also much involved in ceremonies of initiation.

Adrian Boshier's first encounter with a snake scared him badly, but it set an important precedent. It gave him a taste for further involvement with an animal that lies at the center of much African mythology. He responded by catching other less formidable snakes that came his way, at first out of simple curiosity, but soon because he couldn't resist it. He began deliberately looking for snakes, lifting flat stones on the hillsides, digging his way into termite mounds, beating bushes along the margins of streams, learning where each species was most likely to be found.

In the beginning Boshier caught snakes for the simple thrill of doing so, enjoying the triumph of capture and then letting them go. But before long he learned that medical laboratories that produced antidotes to snakebite would pay well for certain species. So he turned professional. It was an important step for Boshier, because it gave him a label and changed his life. One day he was a crazy kid wandering aimlessly in the bush; and the next, despite the fact that he continued to behave in precisely the same way, he was a man with a profession, earning money, doing something that people could appreciate.

Boshier learned right away that something strange happens to a snake as soon as it is caught: it never again displays the ferocity and desperation of the first wild battle to avoid being captured or killed, and can rarely be persuaded to pose aggressively for a photograph. It is almost as though its spirit has been broken. All those who catch snakes know that most become quite quickly accustomed to being handled and Adrian Boshier, with his flair for the dramatic, never missed a chance to perform. One of his most telling displays was an early one, with the largest snake in Africa.

An adult python may be more than twenty feet long, weigh up to a hundred pounds and have a girth as great as a man's waist. Pythons either lie in wait underwater, or in ambush along a well-used game trail, from where they make lightning strikes with a formidable array of curved teeth, then anchor onto their prey, constricting it to death. The strike is usually a seizing movement, but the blow of such a muscular head lands with sledgehammer force and is quite capable of laying out a fairly large animal. A python's normal diet consists of hares, monkeys, small antelope, and wild pigs, but there is no reason why a fully

grown snake should not consume an unwary novice her-
petologist.

The first time Boshier saw a python, it was so big that he
almost failed to recognize it. Then he noticed that the tree trunk
in his path was moving. He stood entranced as yard after yard
flowed by. It was unbelievable; somewhere was a head and, at
some stage still to come, a tail. And in between, more snake than
he would have thought possible.

When he plunged into the undergrowth in search of its
head, the python began to coil its body. This seemed an undesir-
able situation, so he put his stick across its back and made a grab
for its head. It was then that Boshier learned the difference
between the strength of a snake that relies on poison, and one
that depends on its muscle for a living. He was jerked right off
his feet and forced to cling to its neck with both hands, whereupon it promptly behaved like a python and began to engulf him
in its coils.

Boshier released one hand and tried to pull free, but could
not even get a grip on the broad body. Then he tried unwinding
the snake and found to his relief that this worked. Python seem
to be unable to resist a strong centripetal force. As fast as it threw
its coils around him, he unwound them. And there they remained in an animated embrace.

"We became acquainted," he said later. "We really did!"

After an hour of action, the python began to relax and
Boshier released the pressure on its neck. He watched carefully
for any sly maneuvers, but the snake lay without resistance.
Boshier felt so certain of this change in attitude that he even
stroked it. And it seemed to settle itself more comfortably, half of
its enormous length cradled in his arms.

He wondered what to do next. The bags he had with him
were far too small. He decided that he needed help, but the
nearest village was more than a mile away. Stroking it for reas-
surance (his own as much as the snake's), he began to gather up
its coils, draping the python's body about his own—doing deliberately that which he had so recently fought to prevent.

The python seemed to like it! They set off together, in this
odd embrace, and Boshier soon discovered that the snake was

extremely heavy. By the time they reached the village, he was exhausted. But help was a little hard to find. A fourteen-foot python is very thick and when draped around a skinny human, not much of the latter is visible. The sight was more than even the strongest hearts in the village could stand. Evacuation was virtually instantaneous.

Standing there in the empty village, Boshier realized the futility of trying to hold on to his prize. So he staggered off into the bush again and, at a safe distance from the settlement, unwrapped his acquiescent burden. It slipped quietly away, but a legend had been born.

Boshier later heard several wildly different accounts of how he had "attacked" the village with the Great Serpent itself riding on his back. And with each telling, the size of the snake and its ferocity grew. In the minds of the people, he was beginning to be associated with the reptiles and given some of their attributes. He was being identified with his totem as a Snake Man. And Adrian Boshier was never loath to capitalize on this reputation.

As he traveled about, catching snakes for sale, he was always ready to stop in a village and hold an impromptu show. He would haul out his captives one by one and drape them all over his body, allowing them to slither in and out of his pockets and shirt-sleeves. At first the audience held back in fear. But eventually fascination would get the better of even the most timid and each performance would end with everyone prancing about and shouting in excitement. Afterward, when the snakes had been returned to their bags, there was always food and drink and hospitality.

Before long the people began to seek him out whenever a snake had been sighted and, to his surprise, they always knew where to find him. Boshier liked best to sleep on his own out in the bush and each day walked in a different direction, with no particular destination in mind. But if a village needed help with a particularly troublesome reptile, a messenger would come running directly to him. At first it was just the snakes that brought them together, but later the people made more personal overtures.

Late one afternoon, a number of men came into his camp carrying between them a rusty oil drum that had been chopped through longitudinally. They greeted him with their right hands held aloft, palms facing outward, and then set about their mission. He watched with interest as the drum was propped up on a stone platform over an open fire and slowly filled with muddy water from the stream.

As soon as it began to steam, the fire was doused and the men motioned that all was now ready. They had built him a bath. He was overwhelmed by this spontaneous display of friendship, but nevertheless concerned about the danger of bilharzia, a disease produced by parasites found in all the rivers in Africa which flow eastward into the Indian Ocean. It is produced by a small flatworm that leaves its host anemic and listless with cirrhosis of the liver and enlargement of the spleen. This animal represents an ever-present threat which, in much of Africa, keeps wise people away from the water.

Here was Boshier's dilemma: a little warming of the bath was unlikely to kill any of the dreaded larvae, but it was on the other hand extremely difficult to refuse so kind an offer. He decided in the end that it would be impossible to explain why he, who played with ten-foot snakes, was frightened by a microscopic worm. So he bathed.

The following evening the men reappeared and prepared another bath, and so on for every day he spent in the vicinity of that village. It soon became a luxury, something which both he and the village looked forward to. They would retire as soon as he undressed and leave him there to soak, looking like a hapless missionary caught in a cannibal pot.

One evening, however, he became a little irritated by the number of people who were lurking in the bushes, checking to see whether he was really white all over. Each night the number had increased as word of the phenomenon spread, until it seemed that the entire tribe was gathered there in the undergrowth. He picked up a stone and, without aiming at anyone in particular, hurled it into the trees. A howl announced that he had scored a hit and there was a flurry as the audience fled in all directions.

Later that night he woke to the sound of someone approaching. A voice asked for permission to enter the camp and two men came out of the dark. One was obviously in great pain. The other explained that this man had been bitten by a snake and must have immediate attention. Boshier asked about the circumstances and the nature of the snake and it soon emerged that the stricken individual was the one that he had hit with his random missile earlier in the evening. The stone had struck the man on the thigh, but by the time it hit, had turned into a poisonous snake, and now the victim was bound to die.

Boshier realized that, having apparently "put the venom" into the unfortunate man, he could as easily remove it. He laid his hands on the site of the "bite," explained that he was drawing the poison out, and then went on to work over the entire body, finally expressing firmly his confidence that not a trace of the toxin remained.

Recovery was immediate, thanks were profuse, and there were no further intrusions.

Before long, stories about the "mad Englishman" and his snakes began to spread from the Africans to white farms nearby. On one of these farms Adrian had an encounter that was to become legendary.

The mamba is justifiably the most feared snake in Africa. It is often over ten feet long, swift, and invariably aggressive. It is highly alert and any untoward movement or sound induces the snake to assume its strike position, with head raised well off the ground, mouth slightly agape, and tongue flickering from side to side. It can strike rapidly in almost any direction, producing an ominous, hollow-sounding hiss as it attacks, lunging high enough off the ground to hit a man on horseback. The venom is neurotoxic, paralyzing the nerves, collapsing the lungs, and stopping the heart. Two drops is a fatal dose.

Because of its alarming reputation, nine out of every ten large snakes seen in Africa are said to be, according to their color, either black or green mambas. As very few actually are, all snake catchers learn to be skeptical of alleged mambas of either shade.

On this occasion, the news that reached Boshier told of a large black mamba trapped in a termite mound. (Mambas in fact, often make permanent homes in burrows or abandoned termite hills and return to these between expeditions in search of food or a mate.) So Boshier went to investigate.

The termite mound was riddled with holes, all of them

blocked with stones. There was no doubt that any large snake that happened to be inside the old fortress was well and truly trapped. Standing beside the mound was a man who had done the trapping, a weather-beaten black veteran who described the snake and said that he knew this particular animal well. It was definitely a mamba, one with an evil reputation in the area, known to be unusually aggressive, even for its kind.

While they talked, other people began to arrive. A hundred or more black laborers came up from the tobacco lands nearby and, before long, trucks and cars filled with local white farmers and ranchers, most of them sitting securely behind rolled-up windows, formed up in a semicircle around the mound. The farmer who owned the land had called up all his neighbors and invited them over to watch the Englishman try to catch a mamba.

"I was surrounded by the largest audience anyone ever had while catching a lethal snake," Boshier later reported.

One of the vehicles parked closest to the scene bristled with armor, including a double-barreled shotgun pointed ominously in his direction. The occupants promised that, if the snake should bite, they would shoot both him and the mamba—the catcher in order to prevent any unnecessary suffering and the snake out of revenge.

Boshier was able, only with difficulty, to persuade them to put their arms away.

He then turned to the people gathered at a cautious distance and said he needed one man to stand beside him with a stick, while he used a pickax to demolish the mound. At first no one moved, then the same old man who had trapped the snake stepped forward. He promised to hold his ground and not run away, so the digging began. Boshier had just demolished the tough outer shell of the mound when the pick sank deeply into otherwise solid clay. Pulling hard on the handle, he displaced a large panel of earth, which dropped out leaving a window into an internal cavity. As the dust settled, he could see the heaped-up coils of a long snake and on top, an unmistakable narrow, steep-sided head with a hard dark eye, the pupil edged with silver.

"It was a mamba alright, a black one and as big as any I had ever seen."

He coaxed the farmer from the safety of a truck to see this

snake in its refuge. It lay there with its long forked tongue flickering, sensing every vibration, fixing them with its glittering eye.

"It was extraordinarily evil. I don't normally feel that way about snakes, but this one was something different."

The farmer felt it too, for after staring at it in fascination for a while, he whispered, "Man, nobody can catch that snake. It can't be caught. Let me shoot it."

Although he tended to agree, Adrian Boshier hustled the man back to his truck and returned to the mound. The mamba followed his movements with a cold and deadly stare and he began to feel uncomfortable. An enormous force emanated from that snake. It was like no other he had ever experienced.

Eventually he summoned up all his nerve and slowly extended his stick toward it. The snake doubled back its neck, opened its jaws wide to show the dark bluish lining of the mouth, and produced a deep, eerie hiss that filled the cavity in the mound.

"I glanced at the old man who, with great courage, still stood beside me. He too was transfixed by this snake, by the power and the sense of pure evil which it generated."

He tried to pin the head down with his stick, but after a few tussles, the mamba slid down a hole that led to a deeper chamber. When several feet of snake had disappeared, Boshier stuck his hand into the hollow and grabbed its tail. All he got for this piece of daring was a handful of dead skin that the snake was in the process of shedding. Handing the stick back to the old man, he took up the pickax and once more attacked the mound. At length, the opening of a second cavity appeared and simultaneously the furious head and neck of the mamba reared up through the dust and rubble and began striking wildly.

"I grabbed the stick from my companion and entered into the fiercest battle with a snake that I have ever experienced. Rearing up to my own height, the mamba attacked with absolute fury, jaws agape and fangs cleaving the air as I leaped from side to side. I was completely oblivious of the audience. All my world at that moment was filled with a long black body, hissing and lashing at me."

When the snake hesitated after one forceful lunge, Boshier

knew that his chance had come. He rushed at it, hooked it just under the raised neck, and carrying the charge through, forced it back and down until he had it pinned to the ground. Then, without giving it a chance to recover, he grasped it behind the head.

The snake erupted in rage. Flinging out its coils, it fought and strained and several times he was afraid that it would wrench its head from his grasp, even though he was holding it with both hands and exerting all his strength. He was acutely aware that if it did break free, there was no one who could save him.

"Just at the point where I became convinced that the snake was going to outlast me, it weakened and the battle was won. I hustled it into my waiting sack."

One by one the farmers climbed out of their vehicles and the postgame discussion began. An old black man came up to him and said with conviction that this was no ordinary snake, but one with a great and terrible spirit. And while everyone was milling about comparing notes, a lone figure appeared from the bush to ask what all the fuss was about.

Everyone turned to the old man who, with no further encouragement, launched into a wonderfully vivid account of the whole affair. He began by telling simply how he had passed the spot that morning just as the mamba was returning to its lair and how he had trapped it there. But, as the story progressed and a circle formed around him, the old man began to reenact the scenes with great skill and drama. Not only did he assume both human roles, but he also took the part of the snake, rearing up out of the mound and striking. Each time he lunged forward with his mouth open, the members of the crowd fell back and raised their arms and roared.

When the snake made its final attack, the catcher, in a nice bit of artistic license, nonchalantly took hold of its neck barehanded in midstrike. A great triumphant shout filled the air. As the old man stood there, proudly holding up the imaginary mamba, the crowed began a rhythmic chant in which Boshier, for the first time, heard the name *Rradinoga*—father of snakes.

From that day on Rradinoga was his name. It was a name whose fame preceded him across the land, a name that acknowledged Boshier's special powers and a growing belief that he and the snakes and the spirits of the snakes were all one.

The Africans still talk about the way in which he and snakes so often arrived at a village together; it was considered strange and unusual for one to be seen without the other.

But the reputation that grew up around Boshier also produced a great deal of ambivalence. He was made welcome as a man with *moya*, with spirit; but he was held in superstitious awe, like the Great Serpent itself. On one occasion, the rumor that he was coming and that he was angry was enough to shut down a whole street full of shops for the day. For better or for worse, the name was his and only his. Adrian Boshier had come of age. Rradinoga had arrived.

Bolata—

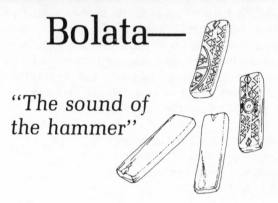

"The sound of the hammer"

Boshier could hear the sound of stone on stone . . . and the song of a woman grinding:

> *You cannot buy a river,*
> *Whom do you know that owns one?*
> *You cannot eat the child of the river,*
> *Tomorrow it will be gone.*

Maize or sorghum forms the staple diet of most people in Africa and each day it has to be ground into a fine meal to prepare *bogobe* porridge. This is woman's work. From childhood all young girls are trained in the traditional method of crushing grain between two stones.

This technique has not changed in over five thousand years. Egyptian statues of the Fifth Dynasty show women sitting astride querns in the shape of saddles, grinding grain with small cylindrical stones. And today, everywhere outside the towns, things are still the same.

In each household is a *lwala*, a block of hard granite or quartzite that has been carefully selected and trimmed to shape before installing it on a clay platform in the cooking area. The grain is placed on this and crushed by the *tšilo*, a smaller stone held firmly in both hands with the arms fully extended. As the meal is ground, it collects in a heap on the forward edge of the lower stone or spills over onto an eating mat. And as the women grind, rocking forward in a surprisingly rapid rhythm, they improvise around one of the old grinding songs:

The birds are eating the growing corn,
As they hold it, it goes down;
If you cannot keep a secret,
Go tell it to the corn.

Ever since he had come under the academic umbrella of Raymond Dart, Adrian Boshier traveled with a sense of mission, dancing to the siren song of scientific discovery. It was a new sensation for him. The bush was the same and his technique for coping with it unchanged, but everything he did, all he saw, was filled now with meaning and excitement.

He still went out carrying little more than a blanket and a knife and would vanish for months on end. Then he would suddenly reappear in Johannesburg, bursting in on friends and associates like a whirlwind, turning everybody's lives upside down with days of noise and nights of outrageous tales. And then one morning a few days later, without farewells, he would be gone again, nobody knew where.

Sometimes he went eastward into Botswana and on to the fringes of the Kalahari Desert. Often he walked down the dry Shashi River which feeds, when it flows, into the great Limpopo. But usually he went north, to the land of the Sotho and the

Tswana, to an area of traditional chiefdoms, each isolated long enough to speak distinct dialects and to develop local customs.

The road north from Johannesburg travels one hundred and fifty miles through the flat farmlands of the highveld to Naboomspruit, where the plateau falls away into the valley of the Limpopo. Beyond this point the landscape changes quite suddenly. Candelabra euphorbias appear on the slopes of red rocky hills and the air is studded with lilac-breasted rollers and the glint of glossy starlings.

Boshier always felt his spirits lift and his back straighten at this point. It was like coming home.

He usually responded by asking the driver with whom he was hitchhiking to stop and put him down, right there between the towns. And he would wander off into the bush to renew his acquaintance with the wild.

On this day, the sun was high and he cast almost no shadow. It was noon, that moment in the day when no dingaka practice their craft because, it is said, even the spirits of the dead are sleeping. Nothing moved in his path except black ground beetles with bright yellow markings that scuttled ahead, keeping just beyond the fall of his feet. Boshier liked these fierce little hunters, who would not hesitate to bite hard enough to draw blood from a human hand, but seldom had to do so because they had mastered the art of chemical warfare. When threatened, they sent up a spray of formic acid strong enough to blister the skin. It seemed as though he and the beetles had the world to themselves, until he heard the rhythmic sound of a grindstone—the music of stone on stone, song after song, because the people like their grain ground fine.

It was a small village, just half a dozen thatched huts in a courtyard surrounded by a low mud wall. And alongside it, a kraal, an enclosure of dead trees set into the ground to keep the cattle and goats from wandering after dark. It was empty now but beside it, behind a windbreak in the shade of a hut, the woman of the house was at work in her open-air kitchen.

> Self-gatherer, seed of the red soil,
> Runner that scares up the hares;
> Big one of the herdboy's country,
> Great warrior bristling with spears.

When the woman reached the end of her praise song, she brushed the excess meal off with a small whisk and began to look critically at the lower grindstone. It was worn into a deep and smooth concavity, but something about it displeased her. She got up, went into the hut, and returned with a dark spherical stone, about the size of an orange, in her hand.

"*Dumela!*" Boshier called, using a greeting that is at the same time a reaffirmation of faith.

This startled her, for she had not heard him coming. But she soon recovered.

"Dumela," came the agreement.

She was a small woman with a wonderful rich contralto voice. Her feet were bare, but she wore an embroidered shawl wrapped skirtlike around her waist over a simple cotton top, On her head was a cloth turban.

"*Re a lotša,* " she said. "A great honor. I dance before you." She invited him in to sit on a low stool in the shade of her marula tree. She brought him a gourd of *maswi,* sour milk, and while he drank it went on with her work. Using the small, dark stone like a hammer, she pounded on the lower grinder until fragments of it flew. He had never seen this process before and asked her about it.

"It is called *patolo* or *kgekgeto.*" She held up the hammer. "And becomes necessary when the grindstone is too smooth to hold the grain. With this I teach it again. I give it hands."

He saw that it was a mottled greenish garnet, quite unlike anything from that area, and remarked that it seemed old.

"It was my mother's before me," she said proudly. "Stones such as this used to be brought here by traders in the old days. We paid well for them in grain or goats. Many of us still use them, but the traders no longer come and you cannot buy such things at a store. This one is the last and when it is finished, my lwala will be too stupid to work anymore."

"Why not use a sharp piece of metal to roughen it?" he asked innocently.

The woman was horrified. "No! That is impossible. Only stone, only this special stone, will do."

As everywhere else in Africa, she felt stone to be something with a life and character of its own. The people point to the concentric layers in a dolomite boulder and say, "There you are. You see. Stones also grow!" A rock weathered into an unusual shape or a stone worn smooth by the river may be singled out for special attention, perhaps even regarded with reverence as a resting place for spirits. But the greatest respect is paid to stones that have been involved in some way with animal life.

Among the northern clans, the people place particular emphasis on the stones that are sometimes found in the stomach of a crocodile, which have been swallowed, presumably, as an aid to digestion or even as a simple form of ballast.

One of these is chosen to be swallowed again by a new chief at his inauguration. It is regarded as the center of his being and authority, "his head, his life." And it is believed that it remains in his body as long as his power is intact. When it is excreted for the first time, this is a warning; when it appears for the second time, this is a clear announcement that the chief is about to die. In this way, a chief can always know when his time is near.

The most powerful stones, however, are unquestionably those that have been shaped by man, that have taken on a form not their own, but something added to them by a clearly spiritual process.

The woman picked up her patolo and struck the grindstone a resounding blow. It rang like a gong.

She looked at Boshier with an expectant grin, but he did not understand, so she struck it a second time, with even more impressive results, and beamed still more broadly. He continued to look blank.

"My stone," she explained patiently, "rings very clearly when beaten."

"I hear this," he responded, "but what does it mean?"

"It means the stone is perfect, it has no cracks. Otherwise it would not sound like that."

She looked around her like a conspirator, pointed surreptitiously up at the sky, and whispered, "*They* can hear my stone very well."

The woman later gave Boshier what was left of an old patolo, pounded down to a sphere just two inches across. He presented this to Raymond Dart on his return and it was deposited in the paleontological collection as specimen SEM 19.

The stone was found, on analysis, to be garnet-pyroxene, a derivative of dolomite not normally considered hard enough to be a useful hammer. But Dart was looking specifically for evidence of hammers in the old deposits, and urging everyone he knew to look more closely at pounding techniques still in use. He was convinced not only that the man-apes were consistent users of bone tools, but that this ability of theirs had been an important preliminary to our later and more skillful manufacture and use of stone tools.

It was generally assumed at that time that man-apes preceded the Stone Age entirely. But when a few crude stone tools—pebbles that seemed to have been damaged or deliberately trimmed—were unearthed at Makapan and in Kenya, Dart began to wonder. He was convinced that no pebble could lengthen the arm's reach, or be as dangerous a weapon at close quarters as any of the long bones of an antelope. He pointed out that a pebble tool could not slit open a belly with the efficiency of a warthog jaw, nor could it split a skull as deftly as a shoulder blade. It would be absurd, he suggested, to think that a pebble could be plunged like a horn dagger into the chest of a sabertoothed tiger, or be used as a container like a skullcap. And pebbles would of course be useless compared with porcupine quills for getting things out of crevices. Before we gave up all these advantages for the sophistication of more elaborate stone tools, we must have gone through a preparatory phase, some sort of gentle introduction to the Stone Age.

There seems to be only one property of stone that offers any advantage to someone practicing an osteodontokeratic culture. It is harder than bone, tooth, or horn. It makes sense therefore to assume that this is the quality that made it attractive. And there is only one occupation in which hardness alone has merit: hammering or pounding. Dart therefore envisioned an evolutionary process beginning with bone pounders, passing through the random but comparable use of harder local stone, to precisional pounding with even harder imported stones. But he had little evidence to support such a sequence until Adrian Boshier came into his life.

The remains of the South African man-apes were embedded in limestone that had accumulated in dolomite caves. There were some dolomitic pebbles in the breccia that showed signs of possible use as tools, but these were discounted by most authorities as too crude and too soft to have served any useful purpose. But that was before Boshier came back from the bush bearing his patolo.

That one little stone and its history forced everyone to take a longer, harder look at the properties of dolomite. The basic facts are relatively simple. Hardness is one of the standard properties ascribed to minerals by geologists. It is determined according to

Moh's scale, on which talc is 1 and diamond is 10. Dolomite has a hardness of less than 4 on this scale and should theoretically be softer than granite or quartzite at 6 or 7. But a great deal depends on the way in which various hard minerals are bonded in a rock, and in practice relatively soft dolomite is quite hard enough to break down the weaker intergranular bonds of granite and chip pieces of it off a smooth grindstone.

The existence of Boshier's hammer stone, the persistence of its use, and the success of an ancient trade in that material for the very purpose of pounding, shows that hardness is not all it takes to make a stone tool. This realization widened the search for possible artifacts associated with early man and has, since that time, produced a number of dolomitic pebbles that have clearly been rounded by pounding. And, to Dart's enormous delight, they all bear a startling resemblance to patolos; and are thus like little lithic time machines, unchanged in form or function through three million years of human evolution. Dart is particularly fond of them because he has always questioned the validity of those assessments of human handiwork which are based only on flaked stone tools.

"The man-apes had a repertoire of tools and utensils so wide that many of them are still being used today. Ironsmiths among the Bamenda people in West Africa use granite hammers and small spherical pounders. And none of these are flaked tools. Their form is simple, but their uses manifold. I see the whole process of pounding as highly important. It played a prime part in human cultural evolution and is one of the best examples we have of that spontaneous individual invention and use of tools which so characterizes human beings."

The Australopithecines had the wit to recognize those portions of their enemies' anatomy in which their strength and fury lay. And they had the intelligence necessary to turn these parts against their original owners. This was a revolutionary advance and evidence of considerable flexibility. But the simple, slightly damaged stone pebbles found among the fossils are probably the first signs of a new technology, one still in use in Africa today.

Passing through the fields, Adrian Boshier stopped in the shade of a marula tree to look for old bone knives. There was nothing but soft sand littered with nut shells. And near the trunk of this, and every other such tree in the whole dusty parkland, was a flat rock anvil surmounted by a small hammer stone. Both were left exactly as they had come to rest after cracking the last marula nut of the previous season.

Each marula fruit contains a large kernel of tough woody endocarp enclosing two rich oily seeds. The seeds are small and the work necessary to extract them hard, but it is a task nevertheless undertaken, for the saying is that *mongo* is food fit for kings. The person to whom such seeds are sent as a present, or the guest to whom they are offered as a mark of esteem, has every reason to feel flattered.

The extraction of the seeds, like the preparation of the wine, is accomplished right there beneath the tree on stones used for no other purpose. And the task usually falls to the older women, who transform it, like everything else in their lives, into a leisurely social occasion. Each kernel is held firmly between the index finger and the thumb on the anvil stone and cracked sharply with the hammer until it splits. The embedded embryo is then picked out with an acacia thorn and makes a delicious addition to a green leaf relish or meat stew. It takes even a skilled nut-cracker two or three blows with an anvil stone to break each kernel and, over the years, the edges of the hammer stones become rounded and smooth.

Looking at one that day, suddenly sensitized to stone, Boshier realized that it bore a remarkable resemblance to the bruised pebbles from Makapan that he had seen in Dart's laboratory, so he added it to his pack. It was later joined by a stone used for braying skin and another smoothed from years of pounding earth and dung into hut floors. When Boshier finally staggered back into Johannesburg, unusually heavily laden, Dart was delighted with the finds.

"Sounds like the damn Stone Age out there," he said. And he sent his new collector directly back for more specimens.

A short time later Boshier discovered a relatively prosperous village with over thirty huts sheltering in the lee of a pair of hills like breasts. The courtyards were stamped smooth and surrounded by low walls stained red with earth and ochre, and decorated with spidery motifs in white. The lower part of each thatched hut was stained red, to hide the marks of mud which spattered up against them in the rain—but the upper parts were washed so white they looked like ice to one coming across the dusty plain.

Boshier came, as always, on foot, taking short metronomic steps in the soft sand. Once again he was greeted by the sound of stone on stone. On an outcrop of hard rock slope at the edge of the village, a number of unmarried girls were busy at the *dina-leng*, the communal grindstone. The natural stone dome was pitted with little concavities, at each of which a girl knelt, grinding her grain with a small cylindrical *tšilo*. As they worked, one of them, an initiate wearing the long black apron of her regiment, sang a lilting song about the death of her mother and the beast that had been slaughtered to mark the occasion.

And all the others joined in a vigorous but apparently inconsequential chorus:

Whose object is this that is being dragged?
It belongs to my uncle and has the head of a rhinoceros.

Boshier stopped to watch and the work went on, but not without a certain amount of giggling.

"I greet you, ladies," he said. And they giggled.

"I come a long distance. And I come to learn of your ways. I know of grinding, which is an everyday thing. But I would know more of the patolo." The giggling and the grinding ceased. There was a brief huddled conversation and one of the girls came forward. She reached deep down into the folds of her apron and brought out a small spherical stone—green garnet, exactly like the others. She offered it to him shyly, supporting the wrist of her outheld hand in the cup of the other, in the old way of politeness.

He was just about to take the stone from her and examine it more carefully when there was a gruff shout and an old man stepped out of a nearby clump of bushes. The girls hurried back to their task. The man was tall and in his thin beard were several white hairs. He was angry.

"It is forbidden for any man to be here at the dinaleng. You must leave," said the old man. Boshier apologized and began at once to move away.

"Are you not the one they call Rradinoga?" He admitted that he was and, somewhat mollified, the old man then suggested that they walk together toward the village. On the way Boshier learned that the man was a traditional custodian of the grindstone. He had himself chosen the site before the village moved to this place. And he had arranged for it to be properly consecrated. It was his duty still to guard it in the night.

"When the girls arrive in the morning, I leave," explained the man. "Too much gossip is not good for a man of my age. But it is I who must choose a spot for a girl who comes for the first time, and make the final decision in case of any arguments. And I must see that no men come to be there. It is a ruling of the chief. Any man found on the dinaleng pays a fine."

They entered the old man's courtyard through a gate with curved buttress walls on either side. A woman came out of one of the huts, smiled shyly, and began to clean a cooking pot. Hospitality and food are synonymous with the people and it is tradition that strangers are fed whenever they arrive. No questions are asked. A good wife simply starts to clean the pot and, if food is not needed, a guest will stop her.

Boshier let her continue. When the maize meal was cooked, the woman scooped a portion from the middle of the pot with a wooden spoon and arranged it in a dome on a carved bowl. She wetted an old maize cob and with this combed the surface of the porridge into an attractive pattern. Then she came over to where they sat and placed the dish with both hands on the ground between them, next to a smaller dish of *mabilo* prepared from ripe wild medlars.

They began to eat, molding the porridge into balls with their right hands and dipping these into the sour-sweet relish.

"You walk alone," said the old man, "like the impala ram. You go wherever you feel and sleep under the trees. This is a fine and powerful thing. But do you feel no need to return to your herd?"

"From time to time," Boshier replied. "But I am happy here. I have much to learn. That is why I trespassed on the dinaleng. I did not know that it was forbidden."

"It is so. But there are other stones, older ones and equally sacred that I could show you. These ones need no praise songs. They sing their own."

They walked through the cleavage of the hills out onto the far slopes where the huge granite boulders had begun to peel like onions in the sun. Gently curved slabs of stone, many feet across, were strewn about. Some were lying flat, some propped up at an angle on those beneath them, others still tenuously attached to their parent domes.

Boshier noticed that several of the slabs were grooved and dented like good Swiss cheese. The hollows were too small to be used as grindstones and too regular to be the result of natural weathering by wind or water.

He looked to the old man for an explanation. What he got was a broad gap-toothed grin. Then the old man stroked one of the stones with his stick, making a soft, resonant sound. He then rummaged about beneath one of the rocks and came up with two somewhat phallic stones, each a little over a foot long.

Moving over to the largest and most battered of the giant rocks, the old man raised the small hammers high above his head and began to pound at it, hitting each time precisely in one of the worn hollows.

Suddenly the air was filled with sound, each blow producing a vibrant harmonic hum, as clear as a bronze bell. This lingered on to overlap with the next partial tone, mingling with it and merging until the whole hill began to throb with a deep, disturbing, fundamental note.

Boshier was standing on one of Africa's legendary rock "gongs."

At Ndut' Lieng Krak in Vietnam there is a Stone Age instrument, a "lithophone," which consists of ten stones that were not only fashioned, but deliberately chipped and tuned by Neolithic man. Together they form a definite musical scale. In addition, four of the ten yield the interval of a fifth (the second and third partials of a harmonic series) so prominently that it is impossible to deny that they were specifically constructed to produce this result.

Most of the sounding stones in Africa are less sophisticated. They are usually granitic, presumably because this igneous rock cleaves easily and naturally, expanding and contracting in sun and rain, exfoliating to produce thin and often inherently musical spalls of stone. All of these natural "gongs" are marked in ways that make it clear that they have been hammered on frequently, perhaps over thousands of years.

Near Parys in the Orange Free State of South Africa lies a granite boulder six feet in diameter that has split horizontally so that its upper part is supported now only at a few points. When struck, it produces a particularly clear, ringing tone. There is nothing to suggest that the rock has ever been moved artificially, or that anything has been done to modify its shape or tune it. It seems to be a natural occurrence and would be nothing more than a curiosity, were it not for the fact that there are several well-worn hollows in the rock, each the result of centuries of percussion—and that a firm blow on each of these points produces a precise tone in G, B-flat and C, respectively. These three tones happen to be the sixth, seventh, and eighth partials of a harmonic series based on a fundamental note two octaves below middle C. Their occurrence on the rock may be purely accidental, but the fact that these musically related notes have been struck, often, and to the exclusion of all other possible notes that can be elicited from the rock, cannot be coincidental.

Someone had found meaning in making the rock sing, or at least had enjoyed doing it. In other places there have even been attempts to help rocks sing more sweetly. Many of the granite tongues have been tuned by hammering in additional small stones as wedges. Sometimes the songs have words and meaning.

Many people still drum, some of them with great precision, on hollow logs. Most of these are men and often they do so as a form of self or social advertisement. In dense tropical forest, drumming is a very effective way of announcing, "My domain extends to wherever this can be heard." At its most simple, this is merely an acoustic fence. But it cannot have been long before the drum or drums were providing more explicit information, such as, "This territorial announcement is being made by me, Big Fred, and my friends." This development led eventually to the sophisticated tonal language of Africa's exquisitely tuned "talking drums."

Man-made drums are probably the oldest of all musical instruments. Many people still make simple ones by stretching a skin across the mouth of a gourd and securing it with a thong. This technology was certainly within reach of even Early Stone Age man, but unfortunately leaves no fossil evidence. The origin and development of drums in dense forest habitats, where they would have been most useful, can only be guessed at.

But we know that early man's most formative steps were ones made away from the trees in an open habitat out on the savanna. Here there were no hollow logs or convenient buttress roots, but there were other perfect natural substitutes, and these have been preserved. Some of them are still in use today.

On several occasions African drummers skilled in the use of wood-and-skin talking drums have been taken out to try the old rock gongs. They are invariably unimpressed and begin with little enthusiasm, but soon find that the rocks are surprisingly well-tuned. By striking direct or glancing blows at the ancient and appropriate spots, they are even able to produce and transmit some of their complex drum language messages.

The best of the ringing rocks can be heard for many miles. They may have been stony substitutes for hollow logs, and no more than that. But the precision of their use suggests a more elaborate ritual function.

Capuchin monkeys pick up and use convenient stones for breaking open clam shells. This is tool-using of a simple sort. But only a human can select a stone and then decide whether to sit on it, sleep on it, throw it, carve it, paint it, start a fire with it, wear it, or worship it. This kind of flexibility is what makes us human, and is a talent that seems to have evolved a very long time ago.

Adrian Boshier and others working in Africa have only just begun to show that the ritual scars which can still be found on many old rocks are surprisingly articulate. They tell of an ancient transition from instinct to intelligence and celebrate an awareness that is peculiarly human.

Leeto—

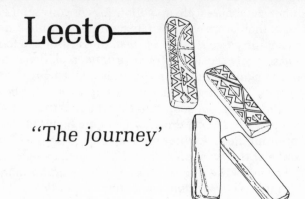

"The journey"

Adrian Boshier's facility with snakes ensured him a welcome even in strange villages, where his fame had preceded him. The people treated him with great courtesy and he was never allowed to go short of food or water. But that was as far as it went. Most of his leading questions about objects of tradition and ritual were politely avoided, with replies such as, "It is something of the old people," or "It is as you see, there is no meaning in it."

Until his meeting with Raymond Dart, Boshier had been prepared to accept these limitations on what he could come to know. Now, however, he burned with a new enthusiasm. He really needed to know, and Dart was relying on him to find out.

The turning point came one day at an isolated trading store in the shadow of the Waterberg. Boshier had stopped for the rare luxury of an ice-cold drink and noticed when he received his change that the silver coins were partially covered with a tacky black substance. As he sat in the shade of the veranda he tried to scrape the coins clean. It was extremely difficult, even with his knife, to do so. Before long he noticed that a wrinkled old woman sitting nearby was laughing at his efforts.

"*Muti*," she said, using a word that in many parts of Africa means a medicine. He assumed that something like a cough syrup must have spilled on the money in the store, but she laughed again, shaking her head. He realized that if this were the case, the copper coins would have been marked in the same way. Then he remembered that muti could also refer to a charm or talisman.

"It is for luck?"

She nodded and pointed to the huge imported car that was parked in the shade at the side of the store. "He is very rich, this *ralebenkele*, because he puts muti on his money that brings it all back to him again."

It was Boshier's turn to laugh. He asked why, if this were so, everyone did not copy the shopkeeper's system.

Smiling, she replied, "Because it takes much money to buy the muti. It is made up by a famous ngaka."

The woman was completely serious about the procedure, and he realized that she was right. "Unto everyone that hath shall be given" was a sound piece of practical economics, even if she had not quite grasped the mechanics responsible. Or had she?

"It was at that moment that I became aware of the fact that even if magic didn't work, the people's belief in it was enough to make it a very important part of their lives. And therefore of mine."

So Boshier decided that it was time he visited an ngaka, a Sotho diviner. When he asked the people to recommend a good one they all pointed to Thaba Bohlale, the "wise mountain" on the far side of the Mokamole River.

"On that mountain," they said, "lives the greatest of all dingaka in the region. His powers are so great that even now he knows we are talking about him. But take care! He hates tobacco. If you go to him with cigarettes hidden on your person, he will refuse to see you, yelling at you to go, to take the poison hidden in your loincloth and throw it away."

As Boshier neither smoked nor wore a loincloth, he felt that

he might be acceptable to the old sage. So he sought him out. At
the entrance to the diviner's kraal, he called out the traditional
greeting and, when answered in kind from within, seated himself on the cow-dung floor in the courtyard.

An old woman brought out a low stool for him and then left
him alone. A couple of tiny children with bare bottoms peeked at
him round a corner, but scurried away when they realized they
had been seen. Eventually the great man appeared.

He was very old and silver-haired, and wore baggy trousers,
sandals, and the coat from an ancient blue serge suit. But he had
tremendous presence and swept into the courtyard towing all
his extensive family behind him.

The two men killed time in the traditional way, comment-
ing on the weather, the livestock, and the crops, and drinking
maswi. For one never enters an African home and raises the
object of one's visit without preamble.

When the time seemed right Boshier said, "I see you, Father,
and I know of your reputation. The people speak of you even in
distant lands."

The old man nodded gravely, taking the compliment casu-
ally, but glancing round to ensure that everyone had heard it.
Then he raised his right hand and brandished a fly switch of
long, pure black hairs from the tail of a wildebeest.

"You have come to consult the bones?"

"It would be an honor."

The ngaka clapped his hands and a skeletal, totally bald,
and strangely simian little man appeared in the doorway of one
of the huts, the one with a small portion of thatch reversed so that
the fronds of grass hung over the entrance. This attendant sham-
bled over to his master clutching a beautifully woven basket in
his skinny arms. This he laid on the ground in front of the
diviner, who lifted the lid and took out a bulging pouch made
from the fur of a genet cat. Undoing the thong, he pulled open
the top of the bag and held it aloft, chanting loudly:

You my white ones, children of my parents,
Whom I drank from my mother's breast;
And you, many colored cattle,
Whom I knew when still on my mother's back;

Know that this is a thing of my forefathers,
All of whom were dingaka;
This is a traditional thing,
Not something I have invented for myself;
Help us then . . . divine well.

With a deft movement, the monkeylike assistant unrolled a small grass mat and motioned to Boshier that he should sit before it directly in front of the diviner. This he did, taking care not to cross his legs.

The old man brought the bag down, held it to his lips, and breathed deeply into it, "bringing the bones to life." Then, holding the bag above the grass mat, he shook the contents out, spilling them in a stream onto the ground. As soon as all the bones, shells, coins, and tablets in the set lay still and their arrangement was apparent, the little assistant launched into a rapid, shrill refrain, singing the praises of the pattern with a traditional *sereto*.

After studying the lay for some time, the diviner gathered the bits and pieces together, spoke quietly to them as they rested in his cupped hands, and then cast them down once more onto the mat.

The assistant again graced the fall with its own particular *sereto* and the old man examined it with great care, then pushed the whole set across the mat to his client. With great difficulty, Boshier managed to balance them all between his outstretched hands, breathed on them to instill a little of his own *moya*, and threw.

The old ngaka took his time before sitting back and delivering his verdict.

"You are very strong," he said, "and walk the land without fear. You walk far and you will travel still further because the spirits are with you. Nothing can stand in your way. The people will not try to stop you because they fear you and your animals." He pointed to a reptilian vertebra. "Your snakes. You need only to reach out with your hand and strike them down.

"You have no time to sit and hear the stories. Your way takes you to see things for yourself. But it would be well that you listened, for the stories teach you things that cannot be seen.

"You must follow your spirits wherever they lead. If you do not, you will die."

He paused and looked down again at the pattern on the mat.

"And there is something else. The bones tell of a thing you must do, but never will. They speak to me with the voice of phuti, the duiker, the one which collects itself for the jump. And by this bone," he indicated an antelope metacarpal with his knuckle, "I know where it is that you must go.

"You must travel, as you always have, on foot and alone. This time across the plains of the Ndebele to the land of the people of the old chief Matala. For he danced the duiker. You must go to the mountains of the Makgabeng."

The diviner brought the session to an end with a great shout, *"Hizwaa!"*

All the people answered, *"Siya vuma,* we are agreed."

And Adrian Boshier left for the Makgabeng, a little shaken that it should be mentioned. It was not the first time that he had been advised to go there and warned, almost in the same breath, of the dangers of doing so.

The people in the northwestern Transvaal call themselves Ba Sotho—an old name that simply means "the black ones." The Sotho come from a common line, but today they are far from homogeneous. They have split into different clans which have developed their own customs. They have mingled with the remnants of the hunters they dispossessed to produce new dialects and patterns of belief. And they have become fragmented by the difaqane or "scattering," a violent political upheaval produced

in the 1820s by the dreaded Shaka, king of the Zulus, who sent his regiments out on the rampage. But the Sotho, and particularly those in the north, still enjoy traditional community lives that are less disturbed and more like those of their ancestors than any other black people in southern Africa.

Among them none are regarded with more awe, nor given a wider berth by their neighbors, than the Gananwa of the Blaauberg or the Matala of Makgabeng. Both successfully defied Boer and British armies from the heights of their mountain retreats. Each has outlived missionary activity and survived clashes with the other. Of the two, the most feared and the least known are the people of the mysterious Makgabeng.

Part Three

*"Blood is heavy;
a man with it on his hands
cannot run away."*

Sotho proverb.

BLOOD

When the Sotho feel that something is special, they say it has moya. This translates directly as wind, air, breath, spirit, soul, or life, but what is meant is more like power or energy, similar to what the Polynesians mean by mana—a sort of force vitale.

A fine pot can have this special thing, but it is not simply a sum of the balance and craft that have gone into making it. If a potter consistently turns out fine work, then he may have this quality in his own right. And if he does, he may be stronger or smarter or more graceful than others, but it is not just a matter of strength or brains or agility. There is no essential difference between the specialness of the pot and that of its maker or owner. That special quality causes each one to excel in a unique way.

It is the essence of nature itself. Like electricity, it is powerful but has no will or purpose of its own. It may come from gods or spirits; it may be produced by the performance of an appropriate ritual; or it may simply exist.

The people recognize it as something in nature that awakens in humans a sense of wonder or produces a momentary thrill. It lies at the root of all transcendent experience, which is not the prerogative of Oriental cults, but is such a basic part of human life everywhere that it must be considered a biological phenomenon.

This phenomenon is what makes it possible for us to see some things as holy. We set them aside as "wholly" other, while recognizing, if only for a fleeting instant, that we are an essential part of this big thing, that it somehow depends on us for its wholeness, or holiness.

It has become customary among students of African tradition to separate the "sacred" from the "profane," to identify some rituals as serving a religious function and others as purely secular. But this is a totally artificial distinction, based on non-African ways of thinking. The most fundamental characteristic of African custom is its wholeness. It embraces everything.

When a man dances he may seem, and even claim, to be doing so "just for fun." A closer examination of the behavior, however, will reveal that he believes this "fun" serves to protect and enhance his community. It is not possible to draw a clear line between the functional and the ritual elements in such behavior. There are few things in traditional life in Africa that can be identified as distinctively sacred in the sense that they can be separated from the rest of life. For Africans, the whole of life is sacred.

Colonial attitudes toward Africa have spilled over even into anthropological studies and left a legacy that often characterizes the people as intellectually lazy and culturally impoverished. It is easy in the absence of indigenous historical literature to come to such conclusions. But whenever a study goes beyond the customary two years in "the field" necessary to justify a doctoral thesis, the results have been surprising. Unusually respectful and devoted studies made by several French scholars on the Bambara and Dogon people of West Africa, for instance, continue to reveal the presence of a concept of the universe that is equal in complexity and profundity to the systems of Pythagoras or Plotinus, Aquinas, Spinoza, or Bergson—while owing nothing to them.

The knowledge of such systems in Africa is carried by specialists, and spiritual enlightenment—the Word—is passed on to the young in ceremonies of initiation. At a superficial level these are more or less complex rituals that seem to involve meaningless patterns of words and actions that are being repeated simply because they have become traditional. But analysis of the detail in these apparently simple rites of passage shows that they are astonishingly complex metaphysical constructs. They not only embody an account of the secular history of the people, but are rich in symbolism that leads an initiate step by step toward a spiritual enlightenment as profound as that to be found in any of the better-known Oriental systems.

As each of the African cultures that has been studied in depth begins to yield its world of hidden knowledge—haltingly and somewhat inadequately when it has to be bent to fit the format required by our own purely literary tradition—it becomes clear that the roots of the culture are very deep. They carry echoes of sounds heard in early childhood; and in Africa that goes all the way back, in one long unbroken line, to the origins of man.

The keepers of knowledge everywhere in Africa are the priests or spirit diviners, those that offer instruction in the rituals. This is not always overt, as in a ceremony of specific initiation, but may be covert in the sense that it provides an experience of ritual without explanation. Both processes are important.

A healer or diviner or spirit medium may know and demonstrate only a fraction of the system, but immersion in a culture means that, in the end, the pieces all tend to fit together and it is possible for an individual to perceive, if only unconsciously, how he or she relates to the society and to the "otherness" in which it is embedded. The mere performance of a ritual is, in itself, a prayer for the perpetuation of a complex reality.

The symbols involved in the ritual may not be consciously understood, but they nevertheless make a profound impression. And it is significant that all of the most important steps in learning, all of the major transitions, are marked by some form of ritual sacrifice . . . by blood. There is no single symbol more potent or more profound.

Phokolo—

"The illness"

There are on earth some places of undeniable power, spots where spirits have their homes. Some spirits are said to live in the center of the cattle kraal, where the dead are buried and offerings are made; others may be found in shrines built specially to house them. But many, particularly the nature spirits, take up residence in the wild: in caves and in deep pools, in the trunks of certain ancient trees, or in isolated outcrops of rock.

The people know these places well and have names for them that act as explicit warnings to casual passersby. Many gloomy and uninhabited valleys are identified by the African equivalent of the medieval cartographer's "Abandon Hope All Ye Who Enter Here." And some mountains are believed to be so powerful that it is not even necessary to trespass there in order to evoke the wrath of their spirits; it is enough just to point at them.

Paramount among these are the ill-reputed mountains of the Makgabeng, which rise like stepped pyramids out of a hard brown plain in the northern Transvaal. They are part of the Waterberg system, standing on an ancient basin filled with the sediments of erosion that took place during unimaginable rains two thousand million years ago. They were formed when bands of sandstone and conglomerate were raised from that early floor and weathered and faulted to produce the typical rugged scenery that now remains.

From the steep escarpment of Ga Mokopane in the east, almost five thousand feet above sea level, hundreds of square miles of broken plateaus fall fifteen hundred feet down to the Magalakwena River in the west. It is a hard—in some areas almost lunar—landscape of jagged rock partly covered by low thorn scrub. With little water, it is a most forbidding place.

In the deeper gullies are patches of bush almost thick enough to be called forests. But up on the plateau there is nothing but bare red stone eroded into bizarre shapes, which rise like antique monuments, like eroded mausoleums that disappear one behind the other into the hot summer haze. The tallest of these is Thaba Godimo, "the Citadel," which stands like a sentinel. On ordinance maps it is marked simply as a peak on the boundary of the districts of Good Hope and Too Late. But to the people of the Makgabeng it is a sacred place. Visible from everywhere within the mountains, it serves as a constant reminder to them of where and who they are. They know it also as "Those-Who-Point-Will-Never-Reach-Their-Homes."

Adrian Boshier trudged across the blistering sandveld south of the mountains. The sand was deep and fine, broken only by stunted acacia and the occasional spiky euphorbia. Clouds of flies settled on his skin, working their way relentlessly into eyes and nostrils in search of moisture. The only respite from the insects came when gusts of wind burned across the plain, blasting the flies away, but filling his face instead with red dust and grit.

As he drew closer to the Makgabeng, he could see the Citadel rising high above the haze. Near it was another peak with the shape of a vulture, looming over the land with its wings partly spread. The country around the mountains was occupied, and obviously had been for a very long time, because the bush was cut and grazed, leaving only the rounded crowns of old marula trees in an almost formal parkland.

Boshier passed a number of thatched huts and small thorn stockades, but none of them showed signs of life. Not even a chicken moved in the heat. So he continued toward the distant heights, with their promise of cooler air.

By late afternoon he was close enough to the mountain wall to see the dark entrance of a gorge and, at its foot, a large village of mud and thatch standing almost in the shadow of the rock face. Aware that his movements were probably being watched, he decided to go directly to the village and ask for permission to go up into the mountains.

Access to the chief of such a village is usually easy. He and his immediate family live in a semicircle of thatched huts arranged within mud walls around the gathering place or kgoro. This consists of a circular enclosure built of branches set upright in the ground and chosen for their eccentric shapes so that, when placed close together, they tend to intertwine. The only proper entrance to the village is through a gateway at the back of the kgoro, so all villagers and their guests must pass this way and be inspected by the elders who gather there around a ceremonial fireplace.

Boshier could see from a distance that this village was of the usual plan, with tall poles on either side of the entrance, decorated with the skulls of beasts slaughtered for some recent special occasion, perhaps a wedding or initiation.

He headed for this entrance and discovered that there would be no need to announce his arrival, for outside the stockade stood a band of silent men watching his approach.

He stopped some distance short of the group and, as is the custom for strangers, sat down on the ground and waited. Nobody moved for several minutes. He did his best to appear at ease and not to show too great an interest in his surroundings. Eventually an old man detached himself from the reception committee and came across to where the visitor sat.

Boshier got to his feet and greeted the man in the formal manner used for addressing someone of higher status, bowing slightly and clapping his hands softly in front of his chest. The older man acknowledged this gesture of respect with an inclination of his head and asked the necessary questions. "Who are you?" "Where do you come from?" and "How did you find things there?"

Boshier answered as fully as he could, waiting for the inevitable and much more difficult follow-up. "And where does your path go now?"

He realized the need for caution and replied that he was simply following the path of moya, the way of the wind or spirit. This evasive reply apparently sufficed, for he was left standing there while the old man crossed over to the group and led them away through the entrance to the village.

He felt very awkward. The greeting received had been no more than formal etiquette required. And for the first time in all his experience of Africa, Boshier had not been invited even into the communal meeting place. The Makgabeng was living up to its hostile reputation.

He stood there, watching as the rock face behind the village began to glow in the setting sun. A gray *loerie* settled in a tree nearby and added to his sense of isolation with its derisive call, "*Kwe, kwe!* Go away, go away!" He stayed, standing alone outside the stockade, waiting for something to happen. When it did, it took him completely unawares.

The ground moved and the air began to throb as a whole orchestra of drums crashed into life in a nearby courtyard. Feeling alternate sensations of excitement and fear, of power and despair, he let the sound roll over him. One moment he was strong and forceful, able to deal with the situation; in the next completely overwhelmed, dominated by the mountain wall which threatened to rise up and fall on him.

As the sound continued, people began to converge on the village from all directions. They came across the sandy wastes behind him, out of the dry fields nearby, and from points beyond his view around the edges of the cliff. And they kept coming, until the kgoro was filled with a large and completely silent crowd. Through a gap in the stockade he could see girls filing out of the village beyond, carrying huge pots on their heads which they placed in a line beneath the only tree in the enclosure.

The drums stopped and the old man who had accepted his greeting drew a calabash of beer from one pot, sampled the brew and then, filling it again, came slowly out through the gate to offer the drink to Boshier, who was now promoted from stranger to the status of a guest.

He was led into the kgoro and given a seat on a skin mat near the pots of beer. The elder who brought him in disappeared and returned with several others, carrying between them an even older man in a sort of divan chair which they set down next to the ceremonial fire.

The old man's ancient head was covered in white curls and his eyes were like milky marbles. It was obvious that he was completely blind. The first taste of a new pot of beer was offered to the man in the chair who, despite his age, had no difficulty in downing it without pause for breath. The next calabash was presented to Boshier. He clapped his hands, uttered the praise word "Morena, great chief," and drank his share, pouring the last few drops onto the ground in honor of the ancestors buried beneath his feet. The empty gourd passed back to be refilled and was offered to the next most senior elder, who took his draft in the same traditional way.

Then, breaking all the rules, they returned the full calabash to Boshier, who discovered that he was expected—"as a special honor," they explained—to drink with each of the elders in turn.

Determined to hold his own, he drained the gourd each time it came his way. Twice he left the kgoro, ostensibly to urinate, but in reality to vomit up all the heavy brew before returning to drink some more.

As each pot was emptied, it was turned upside down, spilling the dregs on the ground. By the time it was completely dark, they had a long line of inverted pots lying between their feet and he was feeling terrible. But he had proved that he could drink like a man.

Then the questions began: "Where have you come from?" "Why are you here?"

He knew that he could not go on avoiding the issue, and replied "I want to go up into your mountains."

This produced a sudden hard silence in which all the men fixed their attention on the old blind chief, who turned his sightless eyes on the visitor, pointed back over his shoulder at the mountain wall, and said, "Do you know that this is the Makgabeng?"

Boshier replied that he did know and that it looked beautiful. But the old man shook his head briefly and said, "No, you do not understand. It is very dangerous there." A murmur of agreement ran through the group of elders.

Then the blind old man leaned forward in his chair, shook one bony fist, and said angrily, "You do not speak the truth. Why do you want to go into the mountains where there is no water? What is it you want in the Makgabeng?"

All the elders turned as one on him, hostility in every face. And Boshier felt his grip on things begin to slip away. There was a ringing sound in his ears, a strange metallic smell in his nostrils, and a sudden creeping feeling on his skin as though he were covered in tiny spiders. He felt queasy and giddy, at first aware only that something was about to go wrong. Then the vague disquiet turned quickly to sudden, gut-wrenching fear. The terrible darkness closed in all about him and Adrian Boshier uttered a small birdlike cry and fell stiffly, unconscious, to the ground.

The fallen figure threw his head back, clenched his fists, and arched his spine until the whole body was stretched as tight as a bow. Breathing stopped and the skin slowly turned a deathly blue.

Then he started to jerk, convulsively, violently, until he was able to breathe again, but only with extreme difficulty, choking and rasping on every gulp of air. He rolled in spasm onto his side, and roared and growled in a kind of animal anguish, shouting half-formed words in an incomprehensible language. At one point he struggled almost to his feet, clutching at the air with hands curled like talons, but as the convulsions took over again he crashed to the ground screaming, with blood pouring from his severed tongue.

Gradually the seizure loosened its hold and he ceased shaking, curling up instead in a fetal ball, rocking gently, still breathing deeply but under some kind of control. The seizure faded and the circle of men relaxed and let him be. The whole crisis has lasted less then two minutes, but it seemed much longer to those who had to stand by, helpless in the presence of one possessed by the falling sickness, by the spirits of the "sacred disease."

Anyone can have an epileptic fit. All it amounts to is a period of disorganized activity in the brain, which can be brought on by a head injury, electric shock, drugs, asphyxia, or even a severe bout of fever.

These fits, which involve muscle spasms and convulsions and may lead to unconsciousness, are not merely like epilepsy; they are epileptic. The only difference between diagnosed epileptics and anyone else is that the former are likely to have this kind of disturbance more often than the rest of us. Epilepsy is therefore a symptom and not a disease.

It is, however, a very dramatic symptom and it is not surprising that it should have become the subject of conjecture and superstition. When a victim is seized by a sudden and devastating loss of consciousness and appears to be thrown to the ground by an invisible hand, it is easy to understand why this should come to be regarded, not as an attack from within, but as a sign of possession from without.

Our name for the condition is derived from the Greek epilepsia, "a taking hold of," but the ancient Greeks themselves more often referred to it as the "sacred disease," believing that people affected by it were especially favored by the gods and possessed the gift of prophecy.

There is still no cure for epilepsy and much about it remains mysterious. Some seizures can be traced to blood clots, head injuries, or brain tumors. Others can be induced by flashing lights, loud sounds, or certain tactile stimuli. But the fits in recurrent epilepsy seem to be spontaneous.

We do not know what evokes most attacks nor why some drugs are effective in controlling them. There is no evidence to suggest that epilepsy is hereditary, but there may be an inherited predisposition in all people to suffer attacks under certain circumstances. It is even possible that epileptic attacks are natural and may be brought on by the brain itself in a desperate but deliberate attempt to shake itself out of potentially harmful conditions. The fits may have survival value.

If this is true, then epilepsy is not the symptom of a disorder, but perhaps, instead, the cure. And we may be doing untold damage by our attempts to make an epileptic socially acceptable by suppressing the symptoms. The Russian novelist Fyodor Dostoyevsky said, "There are seconds, occurring five or six at a time, when suddenly you feel you have fully attained the presence of eternal harmony . . . something which man, in a worldly sense, cannot bear. One must either change physically or die." Dostoyevsky, an epileptic, was describing the "aura" that sometimes precedes, and may even be the cause of, an attack. "It is a clear and indisputable sensation, as if you suddenly became aware of all nature and said: Yes, this is true. It is so terribly clear and such a joy. If it lasts more than five seconds the soul will not endure and it must vanish." Dostoyevsky valued his sensations so greatly that he said of them, "In these five seconds I live a lifetime, and for them I shall give away my whole life because it is worth it." This is an aspect of epilepsy about which we know nothing at all.

Despite the lack of any supporting evidence, we have developed the myth of epilepsy as a disease. We define an epileptic as "sick" and apply the consequences of that definition. A century ago this meant confinement in an asylum. Today we are more humane and recognize that epileptics are not insane, but nevertheless "for their own good" do everything possible to suppress the symptoms and help them to lead "normal," but somewhat proscribed lives.

In Africa the epileptic myth is one that sees the symptoms as evidence of supernatural possession. Anyone who has such a seizure is regarded, not so much as afflicted, as blessed by the spirits. An epileptic is someone to be cherished and encouraged rather than made to feel unwelcome, difficult, dangerous, embarrassing, or even unemployable. The symptoms are clearly recognized as painful, and attempts are made to ameliorate their effects on one so seized, but nothing is done to prevent them from taking place. And the epileptic, far from being a social outcast, frequently becomes an individual with a special and respected place in society, most often as a spirit-diviner.

Adrian Boshier felt weak and drowsy, and more than a little confused. From the pain in his head and the ache in his muscles, he realized that he must have had a bad epileptic seizure, and could have been unconscious for some time.

It was still dark. By the light from the ceremonial fire Boshier could see that the blind chief and all his elders were sitting in the same places, but everything else had changed. They were looking at him with genuine warmth, smiling and clapping to the rhythm of the drums, which had started once again in the background.

Seeing that he was conscious, one of the elders leaned forward and asked, with real interest, in a voice devoid of all hostility, "You are really going into the mountains alone?"

Boshier's senses were by no means clear or controlled, so he just nodded. "You will face the leopards that live there?" Again he nodded. "And the snakes, you are not afraid of them?"

"No," he heard himself say in a hollow, far-off voice, "I am not frightened of the snakes. I like the snakes."

The man shook his head in amazement and asked if Boshier knew that the mountains of Makgabeng were also the home of many strong spirits.

Everyone in the group was watching and listening now and when Boshier nodded once more, there was a ripple of satisfaction and understanding.

The blind chief beckoned to him and when Boshier moved stiffly to where the old man sat, he stretched out a gnarled hand and gripped his wrist with surprising strength.

"We wish you well," he said. "May the spirits go with you. Tomorrow you will go up into our mountains, but tonight you sleep here as my guest."

Ledibogo—

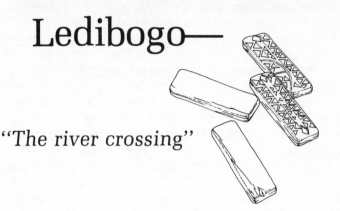

"The river crossing"

Africa can claim, with justice, to be the largest open-air art exhibition in the world.

On the smooth walls of caves and shelters in North Africa, Egypt, the Sahara, Somalia, Kenya, Tanzania, and throughout southern Africa—wherever there are isolated mountains with suitable rock—there are paintings. Roughly one hundred thousand sites have now been described, some of them very superficially, together containing an estimated five million individual figures.

Some of these are the work of nineteenth- and twentieth-century people—of Berbers, Bedouin, and Bantu, both free men and slaves, who produced pictures of their battles, of their cattle, of their enemies and friends. These images are drawn almost at random from their homes or their places of incarceration. Others are older, drawn by Garamantes, Blemyans, and Copts, showing warriors in armor, four-in-hand chariots, caravans, and early Christian symbols. These offer fascinating pictorial confirmation of historic fact, of things recorded elsewhere in literature and tradition.

But the great majority of all African rock art is prehistoric, dating back a hundred centuries or more and providing us with a unique source of information on the lives of Stone Age people. Skeletons can give us some idea of the size of the bodies and brains of these ancestors. Stone tools tell us a little about their industry and creativity. From their garbage dumps and midden mounds we can rescue evidence of their diet, or at least that part of it that did not decay or was not carried away by porcupines or vultures. But of the people themselves we learn next to nothing by excavation alone. And we would still be very much in the dark about them were it not for some of the pictures that they drew.

The rock paintings are eye-witness accounts, vivid, on-the-scene reports that give us some idea of what these people actually looked like. Without these records we would know and could deduce next to nothing. We would have missed news of the introduction of the bow and arrow. We would still be ignorant of the order of the invention of fur garments, leather bags, wooden tools, and revolutionary devices such as ladders, traps, and boats. We might never have come to appreciate how a bow could be used for making music. And we would be the poorer for it. With the paintings, all these things have been added to our knowledge. And, most important of all, we begin to gain some understanding of the origins of religion.

The cave art of Europe is composed almost entirely of animals and abstract signs. Human figures are rare and descriptive scenes almost nonexistent. Prehistoric African rock art, on the other hand, teems with people and narrative scenes. It is alive with animals, humans, and mythological mixtures of the two. All are involved with, or superimposed on, each other in meaningful ways.

Here in the richest concentration of Stone Age art in the world, there are clues to add a vital chapter to our nascent prehistory of the mind. All we lack is the key. But it is just possible that Adrian Boshier may have discovered that vital key in his wanderings among the mountains of the Makgabeng.

The morning after his epileptic attack, Boshier slept late. By the time he walked out of the village into the valley behind it, the sun was high. The western face of the deep ravine had already been transformed into a wall of fire and it soon became too hot to trudge very far through the soft sand. With the *mokasani*, tiny sweat bees, already trying to drown themselves in his eyes, he decided to take things slowly and find a base from which to explore.

Up on the shady eastern slope of the gorge, he noticed the darker shadow of a cave and climbed up the rocks toward it. Pulling himself onto the ledge in front of the entrance, he heard a movement inside and a full-grown leopard sprang out of the shadows and stood glaring at him.

With a snarl and a series of coughing grunts, it ran along the ledge and disappeared. Boshier took over its hiding place and sat there in the cool, letting the Makgabeng take shape around him.

There was still a musty smell in the overhang, left partly by the leopard, but composed mainly of dassie droppings that had melted and flowed like tar from clefts in the rock. Other rock hyraxes were out on the far slope, sunning themselves despite the heat, looking ruminatively down to the sandy floor where nothing moved. The thorn brush on the ground was burned dry by the sun and the only green in the scene was provided by large cactuslike euphorbia standing sentinel on the lower slopes, and by small prickly members of the same family tucked into crevices in the stone.

Now that the leopard had left, Boshier seemed to share the cave with nothing more than a striped sand lizard whose vivid blue tail looked as though it had been only recently attached to its body. There were droppings on the floor which suggested that bats might roost by day in the inner recesses. He went to look and discovered to his delight that he was not the first person to take shelter there.

On the far wall was the painting of an antelope, a delicate rendering of an animal with large ears, head turned over to groom its own back. It was rendered simply in red pigment that had begun to fade and flake, but the treatment was so sensitive that it was still possible to see from the position of the feet that the animal was alert and poised, on the point of taking flight. He knelt down to look at it more closely.

Inspired and excited by his discovery of the little antelope, Adrian Boshier spent weeks searching the mountains for further paintings. He found many. In almost every cave and overhang in the Makgabeng, he came across rocks, sometimes whole galleries full of them, painted in a wide variety of styles. Many of these sites were new ones—new, that is, to our science. He began to make notes, drawings, and tracings, and later to record their location on aerial photographs of the area.

From the condition of the rock and the pigment, and from the superimposition of subjects at certain sites, it soon became apparent that there was some sort of sequence—a change of style with time.

There have been several attempts to recognize phases in the development of African rock art, and to use these to establish a chronological framework for relative dating. Details differ from area to area, but there is general agreement about the sequence.

The earliest paintings seem to have been done entirely in red ochre, an iron oxide, faded now to dark red or maroon. They portray stylized humans, stick figures, and animals in silhouette with no great accuracy or movement. They have come to be known as monochromes, but the lack of detail and the absence of other colors may be due to nothing more than fugitive pigments—extra, now invisible, colors that have faded with time.

The second phase includes more realistic portrayals of both animals and humans in various shades of red, often with additional details in white. In many instances it is clear from gaps in the illustrations, from missing heads, legs, and faces, that white pigments (derived perhaps from chalk or bird droppings) have weathered away. Unlike the early stages, many paintings of this bichrome period show vivid composition.

The third phase includes some of the most complex and beautiful examples of rock art to be found anywhere in the world. Extra colors have been introduced. Yellows and browns derived from soils containing zinc and manganese chromates; and black from the carbon in charcoal. These have been worked and blended into shaded polychrome compositions of tremendous sensitivity. There are elements of foreshortening involved in the subtle portrayal of the rounded bodies of large antelope, and there is often a skillful use of perspective in arranging the juxtaposition of limbs and figures in complex narrative scenes of hunt and battle. There are landscapes, caricatures, elaborate designs, and extraordinary mythological figures, all of which combine to make this the classic period of African rock painting.

Finally, there is a fourth phase, which is clearly historic. This includes subjects such as horses, guns, ships, and figures in brimmed hats that are recognizably European. There is a greater use of white and black at the expense of the more traditional hues of red. Unlike the fast polychrome colors, the white pigment is unstable and rubs off on the hand, with the result that paintings of this style have deteriorated so badly it was once assumed they represented the earliest series. But this decay is clearly the result of a decline in the technology of the artists, and the lack of an adequate binding medium. It has come to be known as the late white phase.

This is the "official" version of the phases of African rock art, but workers in the field find that nothing is ever so simple.

One of the ancient galleries rediscovered by Adrian Boshier consisted of a fifteen-foot panel of smooth wall in an overhang covered with paintings, in some places four or five subjects deep. This confusion was dominated by a line of twenty tall human figures with spears, bows, and white-tipped arrows. Each wears a headdress of white tassles, and scattered around them are eland, giraffe, impala, kudu, and jackal.

Boshier called this "Warrior Cave." Later he said, "I found positions where monochrome and bichrome animals had been superimposed on parts of the bichromatic warriors. There are also shaded polychrome impala painted over bichrome kudu in the usual way, but right next to these is a shaded polychrome kudu, on top of which lies a bichrome antelope, and overlying both is a monochromatic red jackal—the exact opposite of the accepted sequence."

It seemed likely that the four general stylistic phases were complicated by conventions that dictated that one style be used for a particular subject, at the same time as a different style was used for another subject in the same scene. "From the condition of pigments on the mural," said Boshier, "I felt certain that at least one of the bichrome warriors was directly involved with a polychrome eland, and that both the man and the antelope had been painted by the same artist at the same time."

Taken as a whole, the big mural was a bewildering sight. Painting after painting had been superimposed on the rock until the face was covered with a multitude of apparently conflicting scenes and images. The figures varied not only in subject, but also in style and size. They were placed at so many different levels and angles that it was difficult for Boshier to see any clear scenic or conceptual relationship.

"I knew from papers Dart had given me to read that there were experts who suggested that the crowding of images in complex murals was due to lack of space. But in this case, at least, that was patently absurd. Many of the superimpositions occurred on the edge of large open areas of rock. I wondered if the overlays were not perhaps produced for purely aesthetic reasons, but I could see so many examples of compositional blunders, such as antelope with human legs dangling from their bellies, that this too seemed unlikely. I had also read theories which suggested that cave artists chose to paint over existing paintings because the surface was already primed; or that the artists worked in such bad light that they hadn't noticed the earlier works. But in this brightly lit shelter, which contained huge areas of beautiful smooth rock that had never been touched, such explanations seemed to me to be very farfetched. I wondered if those who put them forward had ever seen a large painted shelter in the field."

It was obvious to Boshier that the many and varied motifs in the "Warrior Cave" had not been placed at random, but were arranged according to a clear and premeditated system. There was nothing arbitrary about the apparently chaotic pattern of superimposition. There was a pattern; one in which the artists exercised a deliberate preference. They were using, it seemed, some sort of symbolic syntax. Eland, for instance, were more often superimposed on human figures than vice versa. There was a marked preference for painting animals over human beings, and a clear and apparently intentional avoidance of painting human beings over animals.

The classical theories about rock art suggest that it was either simply a matter of aesthetics—"art for art's sake"—or that it was evidence of sympathetic hunting magic. Art pour l'art remains a popular explanation because of the obviously high aesthetic standard of so much of the African work. Antelopes are delicately shaded and sensitively drawn. Humans are shown full of vigor and vitality, hunting, dancing, and fighting. The detail in all the better paintings is exquisite. A simple admiration of beauty for its own sake, however, cannot explain why there should have been such very definite rules governing the way in which subjects were deliberately chosen and superimposed. There is equally little evidence to support the notion of hunting magic—of an attempt to secure a particular kind of prey by trapping its spirit or essence in a painting done prior to the hunt.

Most illustrated books on rock art understandably try to demonstrate the variety in the paintings. But when a particular site, such as Boshier's "Warrior Cave," is examined in detail, it soon becomes apparent that the artists who worked there were being highly selective and repetitive in their choice of subjects. They did not show the animals that were most common in their environment, nor the ones most sought after for food or most often represented in their diet. Despite the frequency of their inclusion in the mural, eland have never been common in the Makgabeng. On the other hand, elephant and hippopotamus were abundant there, but not one of these large and dramatic animals appears in the painting.

Boshier decided that it was reasonable to conclude that the rock art was essentially symbolic, that much of it had a ritual role which, if we only understood it, could tell us a great deal about the origins of religion. And if this was so, then the "Warrior Cave" and other comparable sites were valuable clues to the birth of the modern mind. They might represent the best, maybe even the only, evidence we are ever likely to have for the manner in which our species crossed the Rubicon of consciousness and became worshipful animals, truly human.

Boshier went on searching for further murals and each time he came across a new painting he would sit and look at it for hours on end, relishing the contact, enjoying the notion that nothing but time stood between him and the artists. He lived, as they must have done, in the caves. He slept, as they probably did, on beds of matted grass or directly on the ground. And he ate, as they did, whatever could be caught or found.

For months he wandered from cave to cave, squeezing in and out of crevices in the rock, exploring every shelter and overhang. In many he found paintings. Some were warm, shaded polychromes of animals at rest; others depicted vibrant social scenes of groups of people walking together, running toward or away from eland, lions, and crocodiles.

One day, while searching along the top of a cliff face, Boshier saw far below a square granite boulder the size of a house. Leaning up against it, forming a tentlike shelter, was an enormous spall of exfoliated rock. He climbed down and found that it contained a bizarre and colorful scene. On the inside of the loose slab was a superb shaded polychrome impala. And facing it, apparently actually kissing it, was a twelve-inch figure unlike any recorded before. It was humanoid, but with a feline tail and testicles. The basic color was whitish, but the light right side of this strange being's body was decorated in crimson and black stripes, and the dark left side in yellow and burnt sienna. On the face was what appeared to be a mask with eye holes picked out in crimson. And on the head a white turban, a little like a bishop's miter, banded in yellow ochre.

This being, whom Boshier dubbed "The Witchdoctor," was poised on the ball of his right foot in a balletic stance, with the right hand reaching out gently to cup the impala's head. The antelope, apparently a female, was stretching forward with its neck so that it came to meet the mask mouth to mouth. Both figures were worked in the same pigments, apparently by the same artist at the same time. They had weathered equally and it seemed clear that the relationship was intended. They were sharing breath. And, almost as though in direct response, a pair of eyes showed bright and clear in a dark uterine patch inside the antelope's belly.

Boshier was beginning to be aware of the symbolic importance and the mythical content of the paintings he found, but their meaning remained obscure. He realized that his only chance of breaking the code was to find someone still alive who was heir to the tradition from which the myths had arisen and who might still know the secrets. He was now closer to the people of Makgabeng than he had ever been to any other Africans, but they could not, or would not, tell him anything about the paintings. What he needed was someone who could act as a bridge between their cultures.

As it happened, on his very next visit to Johannesburg to report to Raymond Dart, Adrian Boshier met just such a man.

Credo Vusamazulu Mutwa is a Zulu. His father was a Catholic convert, but his mother's father was a *sangoma*, a Zulu spirit-diviner, custodian of the relics of his people and guardian of their history.

A family compromise sent Credo Mutwa to a mission school for his early education, but as soon as this was complete, he served as an apprentice to his grandfather, carrying the old man's medicine bags and sharing some of his secrets. Eventually Credo Mutwa renounced Christianity and completed his training as a diviner.

The product of this combination of cultures is a small, myopic, rather portly man. He is an unusually well-educated diviner, with a daunting knowledge of the classics (his own as well as ours) and a markedly biblical rhetoric. For many years he was content to work as an assistant in a curio shop in Johannesburg that specialized in African art. But in 1960, after the woman he planned to marry died in the hail of bullets fired by police on the crowd at Sharpeville, he took a blood oath. He swore to do everything in his power to effect a reconciliation between black and white in Africa. He decided that the best way of doing so would be to break with the secretive tradition of his people and reveal some of the riches in their folklore and oral history, in the hope that this might bring about greater understanding. So he put the traditions and beliefs of his people, everything he had been taught in secret by his grandfather, down on paper. He wrote in English, with a cadence and clarity that Rider Haggard might have envied, and eventually published two large books entitled *Indaba, My Children* and *Africa Is My Witness*.

The results were predictable. He was condemned by older blacks for breaking his oaths of secrecy; mocked and beaten up by younger blacks for his conciliatory attitudes; and denounced by white academics, who could find nothing in his version of Bantu oral history to confirm their own researches. One dismissed his work as "a hoax, full of sex and sadism" and even accused him of having used a white ghostwriter.

None of this does him justice. If nothing else, Credo Mutwa is a spellbinding writer. His work is rich in detail and internal consistency. It does not always tally with the currently accepted, white-authored version of African origins; but it makes sense to a lot of black people who heard similar stories as children. His tales are best compared perhaps with the sagas that deal with the traditions of Icelandic families and Norwegian kings, in which the truth is often more poetic and symbolic than literal.

"To a white man," says Credo Mutwa, "history is not history unless it is written down. He has forgotten that much which now appears in his histories was passed on by word of mouth from father to son for centuries. So, lacking such a written record for Africa, white scientists have concocted their own. They draw conclusions about Africa and its history without bothering to hear the African's own account of events. Then they argue about these theories among themselves. No one thinks to ask the Africans for explanation."

Credo Mutwa offers such explanation anyway. "Cave paintings," he says, "are our archives. Every one is either a record of a particular historic event, usually in symbolic form, or it displays certain aspects of legend, custom, and ritual. These are the illustrations to our oral history."

By way of example, he offers his interpretation of a painting which has been the subject of long popular and academic dispute, the famous "White Lady of the Brandberg."

This is a painting in a granite shelter seventy miles from the coast of South West Africa, now known as Namibia. It was first described in 1920 by a German engineer, but owes its prominence and its name to the great French priest-archaeologist, Abbé Breuil. He described the slender walking figure as that of a "European or Mediterranean lady, wearing a costume that is obviously Cretan, all embroidered in beads." Breuil suggested that she might be Diana-Isis involved in a "kind of ceremonial symbolic ballet," which was proof that Egyptian and Cretan civilizations had their roots "firmly planted in the depths of black Africa."

The Abbé has since been taken to task by archaeologists and anthropologists who see nothing in the painting that need be interpreted as evidence of "strangers" to the continent. They see the figure as that of a young man in white body paint, perhaps an Ovambo returning from a war party, or a priest carrying a stick of holy fire, or a Khoi "Hottentot" specially masked for the hunt.

The arguments continue. Unnecessarily, says Credo Mutwa, for the answer is clearly given in African oral tradition.

"The reddish hair, the straight nose, the un-African chin, and the bow and arrows speak louder than words. It is not a lady, but a strikingly handsome young white man, one of the five great Ma-Iti emperors who ruled an ancient African empire for nearly two centuries. This is Karesu II, son of the Fire Beard, known in our legends for his love of hunting."

It is impossible to prove at this moment whether Credo Mutwa is right or wrong, but it would be foolish to ignore him altogether. His explanation is as plausible as the others, and it has the traditional merit of being a great deal more interesting.

Impressed by Credo Mutwa's work and his forthright defense of tradition, Adrian Boshier took the Zulu sangoma up to the Makgabeng to see the painting which he had dubbed "The Witchdoctor." As they approached a small village in the mountains, Credo Mutwa said, "There is a midwife living in this place."

"Yes, there is," agreed Boshier, "but how on earth did you know?" Adrian Boshier was familiar with the area, but Credo Mutwa was a stranger, a Zulu in Sotho territory.

"Look there," said Mutwa, pointing to a sign painted on the village wall, an oval design surrounding a very stylized face. "That is a symbol of birth. No one but a midwife would paint such a thing on her wall."

And, indeed, the village was occupied by two ancient

babelegisi or midwives. The people normally give birth in their own homes, in a special enclosure made of reed mats at the back of the hut. But certain women, with a history of difficult pregnancies were kept in this village and cared for by the old midwives right up to the actual confinement.

A short while later Adrian Boshier led Credo Mutwa into a cave containing a similar design in red ochre—a sixteen-inch-high, somewhat vulvar oval, this time without a face, but surrounded by a pattern of red thumbprints.

Ecstatic, Mutwa fell on his knees in front of the crude painting. "How wonderful! This place is very special. The symbol is that of the goddess, the great mother, the sign of birth and life. It shows the female part," he added, rather unnecessarily.

"What about the thumbprints?" asked Boshier.

"They are counting. They signify numbers. Don't you see why? Don't you know what it means to keep a record of events associated with that part?"

Boshier looked a little abashed, but the excited Zulu came quickly to his rescue. "They are the number of births. They tell how many babies were born here." He counted ninety-two dots and announced that the cave was certainly a popular maternity ward. *"Serapa bana,* a garden of babies."

"But," added Mutwa, "there is something wrong here. They would never have used a cave like this, even in the old days. It is too dirty. There should be a floor of some sort. Yes, they would have laid a floor."

He fell to his knees again and began scraping away at the dust and debris which billowed up into the air. "Ha!" he announced triumphantly, between sneezes, "here it is."

And as the dust cleared, they both looked down on a laminated cow-dung floor, smoothly inset with granite paving stones.

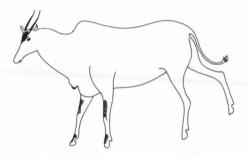

They traveled on across the rugged country, coming finally to the tentlike shelter of "The Witchdoctor." Credo Mutwa had no doubt about its meaning.

"Oh yes, I know it well. This is Rra-bophelo, father of life. Sometimes he is also known as Rra-lehu, father of death, because the people say that the giver-of-life is also the taker-of-life. This scene shows something that is well known to us.

"The spirits have graced this impala with that which all womenfolk are forever seeking, the gift of life. Within her is the seed. And that is why we see Rra-bophelo talking through her nostrils, blowing moya, the breath of the spirit, into her belly. Do you see the eyes of new awareness shining there, staring out from the womb? The father of life is wearing his usual mask and tail, both of which symbolize fertility. But do you see this second figure over here?" He pointed to a human shape almost entirely obliterated by water which poured down the rock face during heavy thunderstorms. "You can just see that he holds spears in his hand. This is Rra-lehu with his instruments of death."

Moving on to a second impala shown upside down with what looked like blood pouring from her mouth, he said, "When the time came, the mother impala gave birth to her young. It was delivered into this world, but she herself died. Here you see her body. And next to it a young antelope licking its own back. The young that have no parents must look after themselves. That is the meaning of this painting. It is the story of life and death. It is what we call *Noka ya bophelo*, the river of life, of continuity. It shows how life is given and life is taken, but Life goes on!"

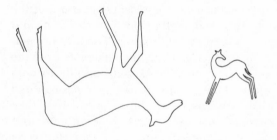

This is as convincing an interpretation of rock painting as can be found anywhere. But it presents grave problems for experts who believe that the paintings were not executed by, and therefore cannot be understood by, Bantu.

Most of the rock art is generally attributed to San artists. The shaded polychrome pictures of the eastern escarpment and the Drakensberg, with their vivid scenes of action and their graceful eland, are probably the work of San "Bushmen," the people of the eland. The rock canvases are certainly filled with images of people who have steatopygia, the unusually large buttocks commonly associated with "Bushmen." And they include illustrations of typical San artifacts such as breechcloths, hunting bags, quivers, bows, and arrows.

At some painted sites, the artists seem even to have left their signatures. Hands have been dipped into pigment and slapped against the walls. Measurement of these prints shows that their mean size, taken from the tip of the longest finger to the heel of the hand, was a little more than fourteen centimeters. This accords well with measurements taken from modern "Bushmen," which suggests that the prints, if not the art, were produced by people of approximately the same size as living hunter-gatherers. Or else they were made by someone else's children.

Archaeological discoveries strongly suggest that these prints and the people portrayed in the art are self-portraits, and not rogues' galleries of the artists' enemies. On and under the floors of the painted caves and shelters are San skeletons and stone tools typical of "Bushman" industries. The internal evidence of some paintings, which portray known events from the time of early European settlement, makes it possible to date them. When this can be done, it can usually be demonstrated that there were "Bushmen" living in the area and that they painted. There are records from the late eighteenth and early nineteenth century of "Bushmen" living in the mountains. As late as 1860 a San shot during a cattle raid was found to be wearing a leather belt from which dangled ten antelope-horn paint containers with pigment in them.

The case, at least for some of these paintings, seems clear. San people appear to be the artists responsible. But the authors of older paintings, and those in other areas, are not so easily identified. In the interior, the paintings are more formal and less colorful. They are executed in an elegant but relatively lifeless style and show a taller people with long bows and large baggy quivers, often dressed in skin karosses and wearing elaborate ornaments. They do not look like classic San "Bushmen," but they could be Khoi "Hottentots."

At the height of the last Ice Age, roughly fifty thousand years ago, there were probably no more than half a million people in all of Africa south of the Sahara. In Europe and Asia there were larger numbers, already busily involved in rapid diversification and cultural growth. But back in the African cradle, the small, brown, less hairy hunters and gatherers went on perfecting their economy, relishing the leisure it gave them.

Suddenly, about ten thousand years ago, the Saharan barrier was breached again, this time from the north and east, and a two-million-year-old way of life drew to a close. The first warning blasts from these winds of change came in the unlikely form of domestic sheep. There are no wild sheep in Africa south of the Sahara. And when the last Ice Age ended, there were no domestic ones either. But in 1497, when Vasco da Gama stopped at the Cape on his way to India, he was presented with five sheep. The domestication of sheep seems to have taken place somewhere in the Middle East, probably from the wild mouflon or the argali. And from there to have undergone considerable selection and modification in Syria, Turkmenia, Persia, and Arabia.

From the start there were two basic breeds: those that provided wool and those that were cultivated for their rich deposits of fat. Wool sheep spread rapidly through the colder countries, entering Africa only in the north among the high Atlas Mountains where Phoenician colonies produced fine woolen materials. Fat sheep enjoyed greater popularity in warm, dry climates and were carried by pastoral people across the Straits of Bab el Mandeb from Arabia into the tempting grasslands of the Horn of Africa. These were Hamitic people, tall and light-skinned, and wherever they came across smaller, darker hunters, there seems to have been some form of accommodation. The hunters adopted or stole the visitors' sheep and in the process also acquired some of their genes. It seems likely that some of them later picked up cattle and other genes in the same way.

The result was a pastoral people, taller and lighter than the San, with slightly narrower noses; longer, higher heads; and a different blood grouping. They traveled more widely than the hunters and they took with them their precious fat-tailed sheep and a culture that included the manufacture and use of pottery. These were the Khoi, who called themselves Khoi khoin, "men of men," but who later, by virtue of their strange clicking speech, were given the nickname of "Hottentot."

It is possible to trace Khoi migrations through the remains of their pottery, hitherto unknown in sub-Saharan Africa, but one of the best ways is by plotting the occurrence of rock paintings depicting sheep. Wherever these are found, there is evidence also of a disruption of the old hunter-gatherer society. The introduction of a pastoral economy, starting perhaps three or four thousand years ago, seems to have marked the beginning of a relentless destruction, now almost complete, of the earliest way of human life. It was the end of a society that had discovered how to live in harmony with—rather than at the expense of—nature.

The trouble with rock paintings of sheep and the somewhat stiff human figures that often accompany them, is that it does not seem possible to make the same simple assumption about them as has been made about paintings of hunters—namely, that they are self-portraits.

There are no written reports, from even the earliest European contacts with the pastoral Khoi, of them painting. But Adrian Boshier seems to have turned up an oral one. In five of the shelters he examined in the northwestern Transvaal, he found paintings of fat-tailed sheep.

One even shows sheep mating. According to the elders who now live in that area, the artists were not San, whom they knew well, but a tall, pale, long-haired race they call "Masetedi." The same name is still used in Tswana to describe the Griqua, a frontier people produced by irregular unions between Khoi women and white or black men.

A possibility exists, then, that the Khoi imitated their relatives the San and carried on the tradition of painting. If this is so, then there is no reason why Bantu, who next appeared on the scene, should not have done the same.

Most authorities on rock art are prepared to admit that the "late white" paintings, the ones whose pigment is not fast, were probably done by Bantu. Many of them show things like trains and mine headgear that were not a normal part of the KhoiSan environment. All, however, are reluctant to concede that the older and more accomplished works of art are of Bantu origin or that any living Bantu could know what they mean.

So Credo Mutwa remains a disembodied voice in the wilderness of white academia. But are his claims so outrageous?

A recent linguistic study of the words used in Africa to describe both sheep and cattle has shown that they are all loan words borrowed by Bantu speakers from other languages, principally from Hamitic dialects of the central Sudan. The implication is that Bantu, or at least a proto-Bantu stock, already existed somewhere in central Africa when sheep and cattle were introduced. This is in direct contradition to the current, principally white, orthodoxy which insists that Bantu arrived only lately, bringing with them both domesticated animals and an agricultural way of life.

It is likely that there were Bantu hunters and gatherers who lived primarily in the rain forests of the Niger and Congo basins. And it is possible that they remained there in reasonable equilibrium with their environment until they too were affected by the invasion of new cultural ideas from the north. Their lives were changed by new ways involving domestic animals and plants, pottery, metal working, and permanent dwellings, which made the accumulation of food surpluses possible and sparked off a population explosion. The oral traditions of all the various southern Bantu groups refer to ancestral homes in the north. The territories of each apparently expanded as chiefdoms grew beyond the carrying capacity of the land, and rival heirs took their followers on to new homes where they too could rule autonomously. So this taller, blacker people with thicker lips and lower bridges to their noses began to pour out onto the savanna and add to the problems of the San hunters and the Khoi pastoralists in the east and south.

The front of this broad continental movement was broken up into three seperate ethnic thrusts. In the interior were the Tswana people who traveled right up to the desert margins. On the east coast were the flamboyant Nguni, who have become divided into Swazi, Zulu, and Xhosa entities. And down the center of the high plateau came the more traditional Sotho. The important point is that none of these were foreigners. They were as African as the KhoiSan, with similar roots in the continent, and they were heir to the same traditions. Credo Mutwa's language still embodies many of the click sounds his people adopted from the KhoiSan; his heritage includes many of their myths and legends. There is, and always has been, a greater degree of mutual comprehension among these people than many scholars seem prepared to admit.

The passing of the San is sad, but perhaps our only chance of understanding the meaning of the paintings on the rocks of Africa does not rest and die with the loss of "Bushman" mythology. The oral tradition of contemporary Bantu, "the People," is extraordinarily rich. In this tradition may be all the clues we need—if we care to look for them.

The physical Stone Age may vanish with the last true hunter left alive in the Kalahari. But its after-image lingers on, burned forever into the imagination of other living Africans, embodied in their life and lore. It lies at the core of all human history. The problem is to gain access to it—to make the giant river crossing of the soul.

Senthulo—

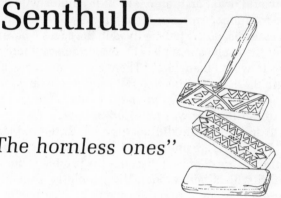

"The hornless ones"

Each day the old blind chief was carried out into his courtyard where, according to the weather, he spent his time either in the sun or in the shade. His council had taken over the routine affairs and left him to doze on his own, reliving the glories of the past.

When they told him that the young white man was there to see him, he was delighted. He gripped Boshier by the wrist. "I have been told that you are living in the valley of *Lahla Dibe*, 'the place of cast-out sins,' and that you sleep in the caves. This makes me very happy, because it is too long now that the caves have been empty of people. Long, long ago when my fathers first came to this place, they lived in the caves. There was much water then and many hippopotamus who kept the pools deep. When you looked out across the plain, there were so many animals it seemed that the land itself was moving.

"It was not safe then to live as we do today in villages of mud. There were many lions and much trouble with Mzilikazi, that cockroach on the shield of Shaka, the one who murdered our

113

people. His warriors were brazen. They would warn a village ahead of time and then surround it during the night. At dawn they would drum on their heavy hide shields with a sound like thunder and then storm in, stabbing everyone in sight with their short assegais. So my fathers lived in the caves where they could defend themselves more easily. Nevertheless, there were great battles in which many died. There are so many spirits who still walk in these mountains that my people seldom go there. But it is good that you do, that your spirits have led you to it."

Adrian Boshier was not used to having his actions attributed to spirits, but he did not argue with the old man.

"The spirits are unhappy," the old man went on. "We know this. But we are confused, because the trouble is not just among the spirits. It is here among the people as well. Everyone is unhappy. Even in our families we fight. The young ones want nothing to do with the old ways. They do not want to tend cattle or attend the schools of initiation. They want to go instead to the cities and make money. They won't even let us die in peace.

"In the old days we buried our dead sitting up, facing the rising sun. If one was a warrior, then we placed his spear beside him too. But the missionaries and the teachers in the schools tell our children that this is wrong and people should be buried lying down flat. How can my spirit be happy, if my body is left lying down like a beast? How can I be happy if I cannot even be sure that the young people will obey my last wish?"

The old chief shook his head in digust. "Oh, the world is sad and the land is thin." He paused for a long moment and then added the last word in tribulation. "Even our wives are not as they were."

The young visitor sat quietly as the old man still clutched his wrist. A dung beetle trundled by, walking tirelessly on her hands, pushing her own little world along with her feet. Boshier watched her disappear around the corner of the hut.

"Chief, there is something I need to know. Something of the old days. Who among you is most familiar with the traditions of your people?"

"That would be the modiša," the old man said without hesitation. "The modiša tlhamane, the keeper of tradition, captain of our dancers. I will send you to him."

Boshier was taken out of the village to a hut standing entirely on its own at the foot of the cliffs. Outside, on a simple wooden bench, sat a man in a makeshift turban, wearing a worn greatcoat fastened at the waist by a large safety pin. He was probably in his fifties, with a light fringe of black beard and a broad nose squashed flat against his face, broken in some long-forgotten battle. When he stood, it was clear that he was tall and strongly built. He came forward, his face wrinkled along time-honored lines of humor in a wide gap-toothed grin.

Then the keeper of tradition shook hands with his visitor—a gesture that clearly showed he was secure enough in the old ways to afford to experiment with the new. The two men sat together on the bench looking out across the plain where several small dust devils chased each other's whirling tails, hurling the dry leaves of last year's crop high into the air and letting them fall back lifeless to the ground. The modiša wanted to know how Boshier got along with the mountain spirits, and shook his head in disbelief when Boshier insisted that he had neither heard nor seen a single one.

"Have you not seen any leopard?"

"Yes, I chased one away from a cave in which I wished to sleep."

"When was that?"

"My first night in the mountains."

"What did it do?" the man asked with great interest.

"Nothing. It just jumped out of the cave, stared at me briefly, and then ran away."

"But you say you have never seen any spirits. Don't you know that was one?"

"It looked very much like an ordinary leopard to me."

"Ah, but what made you choose that particular cave?"

He shrugged. "No reason. When I looked up at it, it felt good."

"Do you not understand?" explained the old man carefully. "Your spirits led you to that cave to introduce you to the leopard spirit. There are people living here in these mountains who have never seen a leopard in their lives. Nkwe is very, very hard to see."

Boshier agreed that it was.

"So you know about this and yet you still believe that the spirits have not been looking after you, protecting your life and giving you food."

Boshier felt a little offended and insisted that he got no assistance in his hunting. He did it all himself and sometimes went without, when he had not been lucky.

The modiša recoiled in mock horror. "Au! Your spirits have a hard time with you. It is not respectful to call them by the name of luck. Have you thought how it would be if the spirits were against you? Many people have gone into these mountains and never been seen again. But you, you come out looking strong and healthy."

The older man stared at him in silence for a while and then burst out laughing. "What do you expect from the spirits? They have filled you with sebete." Which means liver, but stands in the people's minds as a symbol for courage. "And they have taken you to school. You have learned much and gained power."

"What school?"

"You are passing through the school of initiation. The one that all our young men used to attend in order to graduate from boyhood to the status of men."

This young man could see no connection between his wanderings and tribal rites of initiation. He argued that the boys went out for months of special instruction at the hands of old men who taught them everything they would need to know.

"Ah, but am I not an old man? Am I not trying to teach you? A'gaa, but it is hard. You are different than our boys. Someone with your wildness would not take lessons from his fathers or his uncles, and would learn little, even if he stayed for six times many months. So the spirits have led you away to the wild places where they forge you like a spear. If you are to be a full man, you must be worked and tempered. If metal is too soft, it bends. If it is too hard, it breaks. But when it is right, as a man must be right, it lasts forever."

Boshier said nothing.

"The battle is between power and fear. If you fear something, then you have no power over it. Respect, yes. But not fear. Therefore, to understand a thing is to have power over it. So our schools of initiation teach understanding. Those who go through them must first become skilled in survival. They are taught to hunt and to catch their food. They are deliberately exposed to hardship and pain. The proudest, most arrogant ones are sent out on their own into the mountains. And always they come back humble. But they also come back strong. They pick up power as you have. As the spirits intended you to."

Still the young man said nothing.

"I know that the spirits are preparing you. Why you were sent to these mountains, I cannot say. It may have something to do with the caves. That is where we take our children for their special schools. The caves are the passageways to the underworld. They are the paths used by the great serpent and must be rich in spirits whose sign is that of the snake, like yours. You must learn to dance the snake."

Boshier could no longer contain himself. It was beginning to make a strange kind of sense to him, but he was not sure that he liked it.

"Why?" he demanded. "Why me? What does it mean?"

The modiša said quietly, "The hyrax that manages to avoid the swooping eagle does not question the ability or the intentions of the eagle. If he does, the next one will get him. The lessons that the spirits bring cannot be doubted and they must not be ignored. If you disregard the experience offered by the spirits, you will fall. You may even die. But if you follow the path along which they lead, you will learn. You will gain power and your spirits will be happy."

A small, dark brown bird came out of a fissure in the cliff and swooped across the clearing in front of them. As it banked into a steep turn a few feet away, it spread its square tail to show a series of round white windows in the longest feathers. And with the revelation of these marks, which are as distinct as beauty spots, it ceased to be another nondescript bird and became, unmistakably, a rock martin.

Boshier sensed something of the power that even this little knowledge gave him over the bird and realized that the older man was probably right. He needed to know more.

"Will you teach me, modiša?"

"I will try, but I cannot do it alone. We must have help. When my people go hunting, they always inquire about *nare*, the buffalo, from those ahead. A buffalo, particularly one which has been wounded, is very dangerous and often circles around to lie in ambush beside his own trail. When stalking such an animal, it is best to move cautiously and to ask those ahead who might have seen the direction it took. The young and inexperienced should always seek advice from those who have gone before them. And we, who have followed the path for some time, must ourselves look to badimo, our ancestors, still further down the trail."

Boshier knew that in many African languages, the same word is used for both "yesterday" and "tomorrow." The present is the center of time, but distance from the present is more important than direction. Past and future are not seen as opposites, merely as more remote forms of the present. This makes the ancestors very real, and well capable of exerting a profound influence over everyday activities. So it did not surprise Boshier when the modiša suggested that they enlist ancestral aid.

"In the beginning," the modiša explained, "there was Mohlodi—the creator—who made all things, including man, and left his footprints on rocks in the north when these were still soft and new. But nobody knows what has happened to him and no one ever tries to find out. We rely instead on the help and advice of badimo, our ancestors.

"The duty of we who live is to act as a link between the dead ancestors and all as-yet-unborn generations. To do so with skill, we must draw on the knowledge and the power of badimo. We must speak with them. There are, as you know, forms of behavior and address for use when dealing with living elders, who are shown respect, for they too are ancestors. And when they die we treat them still with manners that are correct, but because they are now at a distance from us, we have to work certain things in order to attract their attention. The most common and useful way is that of hu phasa, which means 'to pass' or cut across a barrier, and we do this by pouring out water on the earth."

The modiša mixed up a small libation of earth, grain, and water and showed Boshier how to take a little of it in his mouth and spit it out in a stream onto the red soil of the courtyard. It was a simple ritual, one apparently without logic or reason, but despite his misgivings about mystical things, Boshier knew better than to dismiss it out of hand as immaterial superstition.

He was aware of the presence of ritual in his own life and of the astonishing fact that, despite the lack of any concrete causal connection, it very often worked.

Science reinforces our confidence in a materialistic view of the universe, but even the most enlightened materialist is aware of events (which we attribute to luck, chance, or coincidence) that seem to be beyond technical control. These are the areas in which African tribal people seek the assistance of the ancestors, and though their methods may differ, their motives are identical to those of the physicist who still "touches wood" when starting on the crucial phase of a long and expensive experiment; or the philosopher who deliberately walks around, instead of under, a ladder at the entrance to the classroom where he is about to lecture on logic.

A ritual eventually becomes a reality in its own right. It is not just something you do, or words you say, or the place you choose to perform. It may involve making a sacrifice to an ancestor or offering a prayer, swearing an oath or simply crossing the fingers. The details are unimportant, because they are not peculiar to the ritual. It is the whole of the procedure that matters. If everything is right, the parts of the ritual fuse together into a mechanism that bears no resemblance to any of its components. It becomes a source of power which may not be able to alter directly anything in the environment, but which has a profound effect on those who take part in it.

So Boshier let himself be carried along by the wisdom of the modiša. The next morning they walked out into the hills together and the older man began to shower him with information, filling in some of the gaps left in his education by his late arrival in Africa. He taught Boshier how to recognize those dust devils that could be marauding Tswana in disguise, and how to avoid this enemy in the whirlwind by shouting and throwing stones at it. As they walked, Boshier practiced all the forms of greeting, learning to say when he met a woman carrying a bundle of sticks, "Let the wood return," which would elicit the formal and resigned reply, "It has, it has." And he remembered, when discussing the height of a man, to hold his hand upright because a person walks upright; only animals which go on all fours are described with a hand held flat, palm down.

Boshier also learned practical things, such as the habits of *mbonga,* a burrowing bee whose nest entrance can only be seen by certain people, "those whom the bee loves," who can then dig down as deep as their shoulders to find calabashes full of honey; of *moruti,* the white-naped raven known as "the missionary" because of its clerical collar, and believed to be a spy in the employ of the vultures; and of the taboo against killing a large, velvety red mite which moves like a spider over the rocks and is known as *Modimo,* the same name given to an ancestral spirit.

The modiša began as well to introduce Boshier to the invisible world of the spirits, warning him of creatures that might attempt to pass themselves off as ancestors, and teaching him how to recognize them. Most destructive of these evil influences was one that came like a shadow, like a combination of feathers and a soft breeze which played over one's naked body in the night, building slowly into a voluptuous form that pressed itself against a man in a fleeting embrace and then slipped away into the unseen with a lingering gurgle of laughter. Boshier looked forward to this particular temptation, despite the modiša's warning that the magic lay in the sound of the laughter that enticed unwary men to follow it through the dark, often to their death over precipices.

The modiša taught him a form of words that would put this spirit to flight. As Boshier learned the short incantation and began to build up a stock of similar psychic weapons, he made an old and wonderful discovery. Ritual, he found, provided very potent relief from anxiety. It resolved tension by focusing attention on some positive and trusted action. When threatened with disaster by some force apparently beyond your control, there are only three things you can do. You can ignore it; you can pray for deliverance; or you can work magic through the performance of an established rite. Prayer helps, but it is no more than a request, which could be refused or ignored. Prayer is certainly more soothing than doing nothing, but magic is the most comforting of all. Magic is guaranteed, as long as you get the ritual right. Everything depends on you.

Recent research in psychopathology indicates quite clearly that much of what we automatically put down to chance, luck, or accident, is in fact brought about through personal, although unconscious, emotional factors. At certain times we are all accident prone—walking accidents looking for a place to happen.

Fortunately for our peace of mind, most of us are ignorant of this and continue to attribute mishaps to chance, to "bad luck." And we look for omens that might help to bring about a change in fortune.

There is nothing intrinsic to horseshoes, rabbits' feet, or any other good luck charms, which makes them work. Nevertheless they very often do, simply because they help to make changes in ourselves. Experience shows this and reinforces their value. The fact that our faith in them is misplaced, that we know nothing of the true psychological mechanisms at work, does nothing to make them less effective.

Boshier realized that a belief in badimo, the spirits of the ancestors, was appropriate and effective for precisely the same reasons.

A careful analysis of most, if not all, magical ritual shows that it has survival value. It deals at root with the unconscious forces governing individual and social behavior. By bringing them into the open, suitably disguised in ritual or symbolized in tangible objects or actions, it makes them manageable. Far from being "silly superstitions," they become essential tools for survival—and are beginning to be seen as such by most sensitive anthropologists.

Adrian Boshier's education at the hands of the modiša continued for weeks, during which time he gradually, almost imperceptibly, began to slide into an acceptance of so much that he had fought against for years. Step by step he was being led into spiritual realms whose very existence he had for so long been determined to deny. His fear of this inner world had been fueled by recurrent epileptic attacks which he had always insisted on attributing to the effects of cerebral malaria. It was safer and easier to blame an outside agency for his problems, though there was little comfort to be found in a parasitic worm. But, as he was to discover, there was a traditional African prescription even for this dilemma.

One day, as he walked in the mountains with the modiša, he realized, to his horror, that he was about to have another of his attacks. There was the familiar twinge in his stomach as the color in the hills began to slide sideways along the spectrum, turning from rust to emerald green.

He looked at the modiša and failed to recognize him. The man had a grotesquely large nose and was lit from within by a radiant glow. What was he doing here with this creature in such an alien landscape? Who, for that matter, was he? And why was everybody yelling at him?

They wanted him to lie down right there, but he knew that he must not—that if he did, he would die. So, as usual, he fought them.

He felt himself alone against a terrible horde, who howled and spluttered and tried to suck out his brain. He was terrified, but he was also angry that they should keep picking on him, plucking at his ankles, trying to make him fall. Why should they do this? And why to him? It wasn't fair. He tried to beat them off, shouting obscenities and swinging his stick. But it was no good, there were too many of them; they were too strong; and he was alone.

He stopped moving. He stared wildly about for a moment, seeing nothing. Then the blackness took him and he crashed face-first to the ground.

When Boshier awoke, it was dark. One of the members of that threatening horde was right in front of his eyes, staring at him. He struck out at it, but his arms were held by others at his sides. Confused, he shook his head and in a few moments the darkness cleared a little. He saw that he was lying on his back on the floor of a grass-roofed hut. Leaning over him was a remarkable woman, festooned in beads: beaded necklaces, bracelets, belt, and headband. Over her shoulders she wore the skin of a striped hyena, and her long plaited hair was matted with dry red mud. But it was her ancient face that caught and held his attention. It was the face of a raptor, a bird of prey chiseled in granite, with the demeanor of a statue, but pierced by two intensely alive, burning, black eyes.

She did not smile, but for some reason he felt a great deal better looking at her. He relaxed and those at his side released his arms and let him sit up slowly. He was very tired and somewhat embarrassed to be in this position, but everyone there seemed to accept him as he was. Nobody looked discomfited by what had happened. They were simply kneeling in a ring around him and the amazing old lady, waiting quietly.

Boshier started to say something, but all eyes now were on the woman, who had begun to shake and tremble. Her shoulders shuddered and her body leaned forward as though bowed down by a great weight. With a tremendous effort she shook it off and sat erect again, throwing her head to one side and blowing out her breath in a sharp cry like a sudden exclamation of pain. But the weight returned, bending her over until she had to brace herself by flinging out her clenched fists to rest them on the ground. She screamed. For a moment she seemed to have regained control, but then the shaking started once more and she began to beat herself very hard on her shoulders and arms, making growling noises in her throat.

The spasms increased until she was being jerked violently around, her teeth clenched and her face set in pain and resistance. The woman was clearly under attack and forced to defend herself, beating at her body and the air around her. The hut was filled with the sound of battle. At times the invisible assailant seemed to gain the upper hand as they rolled over and over on the ground. Then she would rise with an enormous effort, throw off her attacker, and breathe deeply two or three times, before falling back under a renewed onslaught.

The agony continued until it became almost unbearable, even for those just sitting by watching helplessly. The air was charged with power and tension, punctuated by the woman's cries, which gradually grew more and more faint as she seemed to lose her strength and her ability to fight back. In the end, she gave up and the battle was over as suddenly as it had begun. She fell unconscious to the ground and lay there very still.

Despite his discomfort, Adrian Boshier was enthralled. He had never seen anything like this at close quarters before. He knew that on any given day there were thousands of people all over Africa undergoing, or watching someone else undergo, what was believed to be possession by a spirit.

In most cases the spirit is given a personal name. It is clearly identified as an individual, usually a direct blood ancestor, but "ancestor worship" is not an accurate description of the phenomenon. The badimo involved are still seen as distinctly human, with all the strengths and weaknesses of our kind. Many of them are petty and are prone, if not treated in the proper manner, to cause hurt, harm, or even death. But they can also be instrumental in providing the positive benefits of health, prosperity, and fertility. All transactions with them are conducted in a formal manner, as befits their status as elders, but the people's attitude falls far short of reverence. Reverence is reserved for the great spirit Modimo, who is remote and detached from mankind, and can only be approached through the ancestors.

The social benefits of such belief are enormous. Information or advice given by a spirit, through a person possessed, acquires an unusual authority. By means of it, a choice can be made from among the total ritual resources of a community. The correct measures for each circumstance can be determined in a way that automatically carries the seal of traditional approval. It is a way of legitimizing and formalizing what might otherwise be capricious behavior.

The individual benefits are less direct, but no less profound. There is a remarkable sameness about the patterns of possession. People in all parts of Africa tend to go into possession trance in much the same way, with the same sounds and movements. The behavior seems to a very large extent to have become ritualized under traditional controls. This structure helps individuals to cope with what is essentially a terrifying experience. They know more or less what to expect.

Possession is really the subjugation of self by something else, by an "otherness," but it does not produce schizophrenia. In most cases it seems to be a genuinely healing experience, leaving the possessed individual with a feeling of peace or euphoria when coming out of the trance. And it seems to have very similar effects on spectators.

When the old lady fell unconscious to the ground, nobody seemed particularly concerned. A younger woman with long beaded hair rummaged in the corner for a while before coming to spread a vivid red cloth over the prone figure. A wad of dried aromatic herbs was set alight on the nearby ground. Snuff, taken from an antelope horn suspended by a thong from the wall, was blown into the old lady's nostrils. Several of the spectators began to sing softly, pleading with the spirits to return her, as there was still much for her to do. One of them produced a spirit broom and began to sweep and swish the air about the fallen figure, running it gently along her arms and legs, stroking her back to consciousness.

Soon she was sitting upright with the red cloth wrapped like a shawl about her shoulders. There was life again in the sharp old eyes. She began to speak.

"Did you see me with spirit?"

Boshier assured her that he had.

"What you have seen is you. This was your spirit, not my own."

He could not believe that his attacks looked like this to others, that there was so much pain and violence, but there were the bruises on his legs and arms . . .

"You go to the places of the spirit. You see them and take from them, and yet you refuse to follow where they lead. You fight with your spirits and give them nothing in return. Not even a goat. You go always alone and refuse to accept a teacher. You walk in the mountains where only the spirits live. You sleep in the caves and travel underground. Could you not see that these were the homes of the old people? A person cannot just go to the places of badimo, the ancestors, without preparation or instruction. There are now many spirits in you, strong ones, both black and white, but you do them no honor. You have not killed the bull.

"The spirits guide you and guard you, but you never feed them. When they come to you, even the *bahlabani*, the warriors of the land, you fight them. You are blind to them and their wishes. So instead of seeing the way of the old ones, you fall in darkness to the ground. This will continue until you have given blood to the spirits. You must kill the bull, but even before that you must be washed and you must kill the goat."

When she was through he sat quietly for a while and then tried to explain as best he could, in her idiom, that it was nothing more than his curiosity, and a spirit of adventure, that led him to explore as he did. But she would have nothing of it.

"You may go on believing that you follow a path of your own choice, but if you do so you will never get better. You suffer from the sickness of the *morutiwa*, the apprentice, and must know by this that you are called to study as an ngaka."

He protested that he was not sick, that he might sometimes have strange sensations, but that he was well and strong. She cut his protests short with a raised hand and began to explain very slowly and simply, as one must to a child.

"In the beginning there was *bosenaselo*, nothingness, a great silence. Then something very strange and difficult took place. There was a voice in the silence. This was the spirit of nothing, a voice that speaks all that we know and see. But of this great spirit we know nothing. It comes from itself, is known by itself, and goes out of itself. It is not for us to know. This is what your people call God.

"God created the world from a lump of clay and himself came to live here with the first beings. They all spoke with each other, like friends. But then something happened, nobody is quite sure what, but some say it was a woman who annoyed him by hitting the sky with her pounding stick." The old woman smiled in a way which made it quite clear that she considered this a piece of nonsense propagated by men for their own nefarious purposes, and then continued. "Anyway, we all came to live beneath the sky, while he remained above it. But when the first people became old and died, they also went beyond the sky where they could talk once again with God.

"When the children of these first people died, they too went to this place, but they could not speak directly to God. It would not have been polite. They could do so only through their parents. And when God replied, he would do so in the proper way, through the parents.

"As time went by, and more and more people came to live on the earth, there were differences. Some of us have become black through long exposure to the sun, while others," she paused and added, deliberately but not unkindly, "look as though they had but recently crawled from beneath a stone. But all of us have the same problem. We cannot speak with God, the creator, the bringer of rain, the firelighter, except through the ancestors. It is they who must speak for us, and when they speak, it is we who must listen, who must learn to know their voices.

"Up to this time you have been walking alone, learning as you would under a teacher. You have learned well, but there are things you do not know and cannot learn without a teacher. This is why you fight with the spirits and become ill. The hospitals in your cities are full of the hornless ones, those who have been called and would not go. No one asks for the spirits and it is not easy to live with them. Everyone fights in the beginning, but in the end one must obey them and do their work."

She leaned forward and scowled at him. "You should be dead. I do not know why they let you live. Others who did as you would long since have been killed. I suppose that is why you are here, and why you were sent to me. It is not my desire to show you the way of the spirits; it is the spirits themselves who have arranged it. So be it. *Rrasebe* will teach you."

Then Boshier knew who she was. Rrasebe is a man's name, meaning "father of sin," and is the traditional title of the spiritual leader of the people. But he had heard that it was now borne by a woman—this unique and powerful woman, the mother of the mountains of Makgabeng.

For some reason he was not surprised. He knew from his readings that spirit possession was most common in the most rigid and structured societies, and that within these societies it is most often the culturally oppressed, notably women, who become possessed. In trance, they can give full expression to their personalities and act out their desires without fear of reproach. They can do so in a way that is positively beneficial to their society. It is not surprising, then, that the strongest personalities in a community frequently come to be its spirit-diviners. Furthermore, all these specialists are drawn to their calling as a result of an illness of some sort. They have thus been set apart from other people. The symptoms are clearly recognized as being different from those of ordinary illness, as being conditions of the mind rather than the body. Among such specialists, epilepsy is unusually common. Boshier had seen a study made on black patients in a major psychiatric hospital showing that most of those who had been diagnosed as schizophrenic claimed to have spirits demanding that they become diviners. Many of these individuals also showed electrical patterns in the temporal lobes of their brains typical of epileptics.

As Rrasebe talked, and the pieces began to fit into place, Boshier felt acutely uncomfortable. He had always refused to see himself as a typical epileptic; he intensely disliked being typecast in any way. And he did not want to be trained or initiated as a ngaka. He had set out simply to explore Africa and now it seemed that he was locked into a process over which he had no control. He resented it.

"After all," he said, "a tourist to England is not compelled to take out British citizenship simply because he has seen the inside of Westminster Abbey."

Boshier walked out of Rrasebe's hut and kept right on going. He left the Makgabeng and returned to Johannesburg to see his family and friends and to talk with Raymond Dart. He immersed himself in the city and its social concerns. He danced and drank and tried to pretend that nothing untoward had happened, but it didn't work. He found it difficult to concentrate on anything and he realized that he was a different person from the man he had been before. There seemed to be an enormous, oppressive weight on his head and shoulders, a burden that he was unable to pass on or put down. He slept a great deal and spent most of his waking hours staring into space, rubbing his arms and legs and picking aimlessly at the buttons on his clothes.

Before long, the strain began to tell and Boshier had a series of epileptic attacks, several in the same week, each one relatively minor but together sufficient to leave him feeling totally disoriented. He did not seem to belong in the city, but he was afraid to return to the bush. Then one night he had a dream.

"I came upon a river and stood perplexed. There was no doubt that I had to follow it, but which way? I decided to travel downstream. This I did, only to find myself in an even worse dilemma when the river divided into two. I took the right-hand stream and it was wonderful. The character of the banks, the vegetation, and the life among it, changed all the time, growing more and more exciting with every mile until my journey ended abruptly when the river reached the sea. I stood there on that lonely beach, which seemed to narrow as I looked at it, squeezing me into the water. I was at the edge of the world, the end of the land. Behind me was an element I knew and could handle, but could not return to. In front was the ocean, gray, hostile, and implacable. I woke up in a cold sweat."

Boshier did not like the implications of the dream. He would much rather have returned to the safe, mindless days when he had just puttered through the wilds, doing as he pleased. But he realized that there was no going back, that he could not walk away from what seemed to be his destiny. He was going to have to take the next terrifying step.

In the mountains of the Makgabeng it was a time of rare abundance. It was April, the month when women ask you to help lift the heavy loads from their heads. Each afternoon they came in from the fields with basketfuls of pumpkins, green maize, roots, and relishes. And there were always bowls of tasty cakes made from ground nuts or dried *muwe*, the sweet fruit of the bird-plum tree. The abundance and variety of food made people forget that there might be shortages later. They spent much time in friendly dancing and carrying beer to their relatives-in-law, laughing and joking in anticipation of the goat, which custom dictates must be killed on such an occasion.

Adrian Boshier also came to the mountains in search of a goat for killing. He went straight to Rrasebe.

"You must have an eye," she said. "Without it your spirits cannot come through. They cannot see, nor give you what you need. So they are angry and give you trouble instead. A goat will provide the eye. I will find one for you."

The following morning they went out into the fields in search of the necessary herbs, principally *mafiroane*, the baboon tail, which is known among other things to be a protection against lightning. Such sacred plants require permission from the spirits to dig them from the ground and the performance of a special praise song. The herbs were mixed together in a deep pot and beaten into a foam with a stick like a whisk that was spun between the palms.

When all was ready, word went out to the other dingaka of the village and that evening they all gathered in the courtyard of Rrasebe. In the warm light of the setting sun, reflected from the cliffs behind him, Boshier sat while an apprentice washed his hands and feet, right up to the knee, in a deep wooden bowl. Then everyone went together into a hut and the goat, a dappled one with the pattern of a python, was brought to him. It bleated, and the people said: "*Magosi,* big chief!"

Boshier took some of the foaming herbal brew and ran it with a stick over the goat's nose, and down its back to the tip of its tail. "I dedicate this chicken," he said, in the accepted form of understatement.

"It is an ox!" they all shouted. Then with very little further ceremony, the animal's throat was cut with a knife. Its blood was collected in a marula wood bowl and placed at his feet. He lifted the bowl up with both hands and said, "I am pierced by blood." And drank.

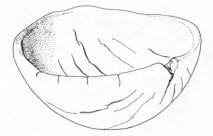

Boshier discovered that although most tribal people in Africa have no knowledge of the circulation of the blood, they recognize it, like people everywhere, as the vital essence. It is not, however, assumed that the heart causes the blood to flow. A tribal herbalist explained to him that the function of the heart was to exclude blood, which flooded in and caused death when that organ stopped beating. It was, the herbalist said, the spirit in blood that made it move, thus giving it vitality even when removed from the body. It may even gain in power, he suggested, because blood shed by a sacrificial animal attracts other spirits that come to feed. And if the people drink enough, some of these discarnate entities may even become visible to them.

Blood is, everyone agreed, the source of all that is life-enhancing. When filtered through the breasts, it becomes milk. When passed through the testes, it turns into semen. Blood carries a greater psychic load, has a more profoundly emotional effect, is richer in symbolism, than any other substance. It reaches directly into unconscious areas, stirring up such depths of feeling that the personality frequently opts out altogether and even strong men faint at the sight of it.

Small wonder, then, that blood is the substance chosen to mark all the most momentous occasions, those celebrated by the most sacred rites of passage—and that in each of these it plays a central role, grasping, binding, and incorporating those involved, giving them access to areas of ambivalence that cannot be understood in causal terms and dare not be admitted as motives for action.

"Blood is," say the people. "Blood knows."

The goat's skin was removed and, while it was still wet, a long strip was cut from its back and placed like a bandolier over Adrian Boshier's left shoulder and under his right arm. A smaller strip was tied around his right wrist as a bangle, remaining there for months until finally it fell away.

The gall bladder was produced and brought to life by Rrasebe herself, resplendent in all her regalia, who breathed moya into it and tied the inflated organ, like a toy balloon, to the headband of beads that Boshier wore.

A huge fire was built in the center of the yard, the rest of the goat was grilled and eaten, a great deal of beer was drunk, and everyone danced most of the night.

Adrian Boshier felt liberated, free at last of the burden he had carried for so long. He led most of the steps himself, wearing out relays of other dancers and drummers with his manic energy. And Rrasebe, father of sin, mother of her people, watched with a quiet gleam of pride in her jet-black eyes. It had been a long time since she last had had such a novice.

Mohlasana—

"The little tree"

In theory, anyone can become a diviner. In practice, the vast majority are women, who are nevertheless known as "father" when they become proficient enough to have students of their own. There is nothing distinctive about those who do get trained. They have little in common and the office is not necessarily hereditary.

"The spirits choose the ones they want. That is all we know," say the people of Africa.

The choice is announced in a dream or vision, which is normally obscure and frequently terrifying. This is followed by other recognized signs such as sleeplessness or excessive yawning, sneezing, belching, or hiccuping, all without reason. And if these omens are ignored, the reluctant appointee is stricken with the characteristic "illness of the apprentice" and continues to suffer from it until the initiation. Training usually begins with the assumption that the novice is newborn and needs to be treated as a child, taken carefully through all the stages necessary to learn how to survive.

In Adrian Boshier's case, Rrasebe decided that the spirits had already supervised this phase of his instruction, even teaching him the necessary dances so that he "quivered like sheet lightning" and stamped the ground hard enough to excite the most moribund spirits. In view of his prowess with snakes, he was excused also from the usual requirement of catching a wild animal.

Rrasebe began immediately to instruct her novice in the secrets of her trade. Each day they walked together through the mountains and she named each of the plants they encountered and described its properties and uses. There was umsenge, the cabbage tree whose roots are chewed for colic, and whose bark is used for preparing an enema that rids the intestines of parasites, especially beetles introduced by witchcraft. The shoots of lengana, wild wormwood, he learned, will instantly cure toothache when inserted into a cavity. And the wood of the mmilo tree is never burned near a kraal because the smoke produces nothing but male calves. Rrasebe stopped in front of an ebony tree and rapped a branch with her fly whisk. "There are other trees, however, which must be burned. This one, mofedisi, the destroyer, is the one who puts an end to things and causes bad blood and quarreling in a home. It must be totally removed and burned to ashes. This is one of the black medicines.

"But this," she broke the tip off a succulent aloe leaf from which oozed a clear, tacky sap, "we burn for another reason altogether. This is mokgopha and from its ashes we make the snuff which we use to please the spirits. This is a thing which is completely white."

Throughout Africa, color plays an important role in symbolism, particularly that related to medicine. The important shades are black, red, and white. Black is the color of night, death, excrement, and illness. White is daylight, life, food, and good health. Red is generally equivocal, indicating a transformation. The red of sunrise is a move toward health, the red of sunset a decline into disease. Whenever a "black" or "red" substance is taken, it must be followed by a "white" one, but the latter can be used on its own.

Very often the medicines may be linked with a sacrificial animal, which is either pure black or pure white. A black goat is usually a scapegoat, killed and buried with evil attached to it, or allowed to escape with the sins of the people upon its back. A white goat represents daylight and social activity, bringing the living and the dead together in a special way over a meal. All the colors are linked with another symbolic system, which operates more or less independently.

"The understanding of this matter of color," said Rrasebe, "comes with the knowledge of hot and cold. Illness causes the blood to be hot and is best treated with cool white medicines, or by pressing a smooth stone against all the joints of the body and then taking it back to the river. Heat is bad for a person and for the country. A man killed by fever, a person struck by lightning, or a woman dying in childbirth, cause the land to be burned and dry. They must be buried right away in wet soil if the country is to be kept cool and the rains are to fall again."

Boshier began to understand that in Africa "to be cool" meant to be calm, soothed, and free from agitation. Ever since his first discovery of a rock painting, he had asked the people about them and they had said only that they knew about them, that they were made by the San or the Masetedi, or perhaps by the spirits. But always they had denied knowledge of any meaning behind the scenes and symbols. Even when he found similar patterns freshly painted on village walls, he was told only that they were "pretty" or that they were "to God" and had no other significance.

Now, after years of incomprehension and evasion, he discovered that at least some of the people were not only very familiar with the painted patterns, but had actually made them or seen them being made. It was Rrasebe herself who took Boshier to the caves. They went first to the one in which she herself had been born. "I can remember sitting here as a child, watching my father work his paints. He would take a white stone, one that came from a river in the south, and grind it into powder. He also ground charcoal and red earth and mixed all these with water, the milk of a plant we call *mohloko* and the green liquid from a gall bladder. Then he would take the colors and paint special signs on the walls."

She pointed to a large white handprint. "That is my father. It is his mark. It says 'I have claimed this place for my family, do not enter or disturb my things.' And that," she indicated a tiny hand lower down on the wall, "that is me. My father made that too, to show that his first child was born here."

He asked her about a simple circle drawn high on the wall, remembering again that the experts had told him that all the geometric art was nonrepresentational and probably nothing more than the doodling of idle herdboys.

"That is *kgwedi*, the moon, whose name means something which is bright, pleasing, and soothing. It was made by the Tree of Life." She showed him a spidery symbol a little like the cross of Lorraine. "The great tree scooped up a ball of clay and stones and used it to stun the mother goddess and bring her down to be his lover. But the ball kept on going. It rose up and up into the sky, so high that the sun became jealous. 'You shall not be my rival,' he said. 'You are a woman and, like all such, think only of passion. You are destined to travel a short way behind. You will shine when I rest and, while my light brings life to the earth, your cold useless glow will bring fire only to the loins of lovers.' The sun eventually took the moon to wife, but only after softening her pride by sending the hyena-of-darkness to devour a little of her with each passing day, leaving always a small piece so that she could grow again. For us she is a sign of growth and all things that continue.

"When the new moon is thin and first seen, everybody cheers, especially the children. For the next day it is forbidden to cut trees or till the fields. The moon must be left undisturbed in order to grow strong. We look very carefully at the horns of the new moon. If they are turned down toward the earth, this is a good omen. All sickness has been turned out. If they are turned toward heaven, this is bad. We say the moon is full of misfortunes."

They went on to another shelter, one that Boshier had often wondered about. It was filled with a sprawling, hectic scene in black and white, a crazy pattern surrounded by spiky four-legged animals and what looked like human figures on horseback.

"This tells the story of a great battle between our people and the Waburu. We hid here in the caves and built walls to protect ourselves, but many were killed."

Boshier remembered that in 1894 General Joubert of the old

Transvaal Republic had led a party of Boers in an attack on the rebellious Chief Malaboch in the neighboring Blaauberg, and supposed that the conflict must have spilled over into the Makgabeng. He wondered, not for the first time, how old Rrasebe actually was.

The paint in this scene was comparatively fresh and she confirmed that it had been recently renewed. It was, in fact, worked over again with each telling of the tale to boys undergoing their tribal initiation. The old men brought them to the caves at night and instructed them there in all the history and lore of their people.

She then led him to a cave he had not seen before, a deep cavern with walls covered by geometric forms, principally concentric circles with a dot in the center of each. There has been considerable discussion of this motif in rock art literature and a consensus that, if it is representational at all, this symbol indicates the proximity of a water hole.

"It is the tail of *phaga*," said Rrasebe positively. "The wild cat, whose banded tail is worn by girls during initiation. This is an initiation cave. I was taught here and teach here now myself when it is the year of the school for girls. It is here that the girls are kept for a month with their legs tied together so that they can move only slowly. They learn the words and the songs, and the secrets of pleasing a man, and then return in full regiment to the village wrapped completely in large grass mats to conceal their painted bodies until the final bathing."

The old lady pointed to another symbol, a circle with radiating lines around it. "*That* is a sign you may find near water. It is *letsatsi*, the sun who eats the water. Rain doctors make such a mark where they pray to the sun. First they walk to the east to greet the rising sun and then they pray, pleading with it not to beat down too fiercely, not to kill the people, but to bring rain and fill the rivers."

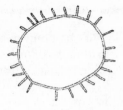

Adrian Boshier was immensely excited by his discovery that geometric designs in the painted caves were not random scribbles, but symbols with importance and meaning. When his training at Rrasebe's hands was complete, he took the opportunity to visit other tribal people and, using his newfound status as an initiate, he was able to discover that the symbols of Makgabeng had the same use and meaning among the Zulus, the Kgatla, the Shangaan, the Karenga, and even the San.

He learned from diviners in each of these cultures that they not only read the signs in the same way, but often explained them in precisely the same words. They were, in effect, using a common set of symbols, a written language, in a world in which none is supposed to exist. What he had discovered was, moreover, a language that cut right across what were generally held to be rigid cultural barriers.

Boshier never had the chance to pursue his findings much further, but in the past few years others have been turning up similar information which, taken altogether, is going to make it necessary to rewrite much of what has been published so far on the origins of writing and the role of literacy in African culture.

Historians are fond of separating culture into a large prehistoric "savage" phase and a brief (six thousand year) spell of "civilization," beginning only with the invention of writing. Quite apart from the way in which this attitude underrates the richness and sophistication of oral tradition, it fails also to recognize that there seem to have been a number of graphic systems that developed long before the four-hundred-odd scripts now recognized.

The first attempts to communicate with others at a distance, in either time or space, were undoubtedly symbolic. A handprint on a cave wall said "keep out" as simply and effectively as a splash of urine on a rock marking the boundary of an individual territory.

Much more complex messages became possible with extensions of the same system. At one point in his campaign against the Scythians, King Darius I received a herald from the enemy bearing nothing but a bird, a mouse, a frog, and five arrows. It was a warning that said, "Unless you fly into the air, burrow into the earth, or jump into the water, there is nothing you can do to avoid being smitten by our weapons," but the Persian failed to read it correctly and was beaten.

In Africa, similar messages are still being sent by means of seashells or patterns of colored beads woven into belts or bracelets. These carry traditional meanings that depend only on simple agreements about the codes and symbols used. They are particularly effective in communicating across language barriers. Our international system of road signs is a comparable modern example. In the case of some nonabstract road signs, which show pictures of trucks or pedestrians, the pictograms have evolved into ideograms which, by convention, no longer necessarily represent the object depicted, but an idea associated with that object. The sun sign on African rock walls, which Boshier discovered to be part of a rainmaking ritual, is a good ancient example of such transference. Other, older signs suggest that even Early Stone Age man may have had a kind of graphic language.

In a Swaziland cave where Boshier once worked, the discovery was made of a fifty-thousand-year-old bone incised with notches or tally marks. A large number of other similarly engraved bones have been found in European Paleolithic sites. It is accepted that these marks were deliberately man-made; it has even been suggested that they were "scorecards" or calendar sticks whose function was purely numerical, not unlike the quipus or knotted string cords once used by the Incas. Recent studies of the Incan cords, and a microscopic analysis of the bones, however, shows that far more information may be gleaned from these objects. The Stone Age markings were very carefully engraved, showing complex sequential arrangements that are clearly neither random nor accidental, nor simply connected with counting. It is now being argued that they represent deliberate notations.

If the Mediterranean examples are evidence of such advanced symbolic activity, they could be the cultural precursors of formal writing and arithmetic, putting this development into the European arena. But the oldest ones date back no more than thirty thousand years, while the Swaziland artifact is at least twenty thousand years older than that.

Symbolic scratches and pictures are effective within a narrow context, but they are open to wide misinterpretation. Graphic signs represent cycles of thought and symbolic ideas, but they are unconnected with any form of linguistic expression. Greater precision becomes possible only when the symbols have phonetic value, when they are deliberately chosen to represent sounds in a spoken language. This development, far from being peculiar to the river valley civilizations of the Middle East and confined to the last six thousand years, may have taken place much earlier in sub-Saharan Africa.

Conventional wisdom sees Egyptian scribes, working in their "houses of light" attached to the dynastic temples, as the originators of the first script. But were they? The most archaic forms of farming technology and religion to have survived in Africa are those of the Voltaic people. And among these, none has a culture more rich in ancient ritual than the Dogon, who live in the great bend of the Volta River.

Anthropologists are only just beginning to plumb the depths of Dogon belief, which is so complex that an outline of their myth concerning just the first few minutes of creation runs to five hundred pages. The keepers of this tradition are the priests, who recognize 256 "complete signs of the world," each of which is given a symbol. These are found nowhere else but in the hidden foundations of altars, traced there by priests as these structures are being built, and never seen by anyone else. They are actual letters, which compose a complete script known only to a handful of the highest initiates. Until very recently even the existence of this ancient alphabet, which may have been old when the Egyptian scribes were still learning their hieroglyphic system, was totally unknown to a world that classified the Dogon as illiterate.

Now there are signs of another such surprise brewing in southern Africa.

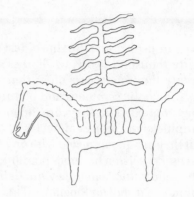

After discovering that the geometric patterns in cave paintings were meaningful, Adrian Boshier tried to apply the same system of interpretation to rock engravings that he found nearby. Apart from being exceptionally rich in cave art, Africa has more than its fair share of freestanding decorated stones. In some of the drier parts of the central plateau, whole acres of rock are covered in patterns and symbols, all meticulously pecked out on the hard stone surface. Many of these are elegant portraits of recognizable animals, but a great number of others are purely abstract and apparently meaningless lithic scribbles. Most have been dismissed at one time or another as doodles, but there is something disturbingly sentient about their pattern and frequency. It may be purely coincidental, but the stylized engravings occur in precisely those areas now known to be rich in diamond-bearing gravels. The suspicion grows that there could be some connection.

As early as 1867, when the first diamond diggings in South Africa began, the miners noticed a curious fact: whenever Stone Age artifacts turned up in the gravel, there would be no diamonds. The old-timers soon learned, when they found such tools, simply to pull up their claim pegs and moved on to new ground, grumbling that the "Old Ones" had been there already. This cannot be dismissed as a mere diggers' superstition because there is never a shortage of diamonds anywhere else in such a plundered "run."

"Diamonds were unknown in the ancient world," say the experts. But in 1974 a digger in the western Transvaal, ploughing through twenty-eight feet of muddy overburden with his mechanical shovel, discovered that someone had been there before him. A pit fourteen feet wide had been dug down through the underlying gravel right to the base rock. And on this ancient floor lay a dozen stone tools of exceptional quality—among heaps of stones which had been carefully sorted and graded and were totally devoid of diamonds. Someone, it seems, in prehistoric times, wanted diamonds very badly. And they may have left their signatures, cut with these abrasive gems, in the hard diabase and dolerite nearby.

Prominent among the engravings are comblike symbols that bear a startling resemblance to a script called ogam.

The earliest dated reference to this alphabet is in a collection of ancient Celtic lore and poetry called "The Book of Leinster" from A.D. 1150. But the characters figure prominently on stones in Ireland, Britain, and Brittany that may go as far back as five thousand years.

Ogam is a simple system of short lines drawn out from a longer straight stem line. It occurs in sets of from one to five lines lying either above, below, or running diagonally through the longer stem. To the casual eye, it looks like a lattice or old-fashioned ladder and could be purely arbitrary, but a closer look reveals sequences and patterns which cannot be accidental.

The most telling are those from two African sites that include useful pictographic clues. At one is a giraffe alongside which lies an ogam line that can be read as R-Z-R-F. With the addition of vowels, which seem to be missing in much ogam as they are in hieroglyphics, this becomes Rai ZaRaFa—old Arabic for "behold the giraffe." And at the other site, a zebra is shown, above which appears an inscription that may be read as Z-B-D-B, which could be ZeB DaBba—Arabic for "painted ass."

Perhaps the most startling discovery of all is a slate tablet that forms part of the professional gear of Adrian Boshier's associate Credo Mutwa, the literary Zulu diviner. This was apparently handed down to him as an heirloom of his trade, and it carries a pattern which makes sense even to an untutored eye. In one column are pictographic symbols that have been identified as Egyptian hieroglyphics. In the second are simple, apparently early, Arabic letters. In the third is the characteristic scalariform outline of the entire ogam alphabet.

If this is genuine, it has an importance to the study of African prehistory as great as the Rosetta Stone. At the very least, it shows that someone carried the Arabic key to ogam at a time when hieroglyphics were still a lingua franca. Its presence as a ritual object in sub-Saharan Africa raises fascinating possibilities. Perhaps ogam, far from being a Celtic invention, was developed and used in "illiterate" Africa, and only exported, along with gold, diamonds, iron, and sacred pigments by early Arab or Phoenician traders.

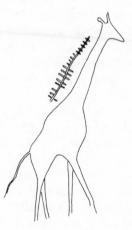

Rrasebe spent a week roaming the mountains with Adrian Boshier and each night, when it became too dark to search for further symbols, she taught him about *dinaledi*, the stars.

"These are the eyes of the ancestors. Widows do not like to sleep when there are many; they want instead to look at their husbands."

She pointed with her stick at the bright star he knew as

Canopus. "Most important among them is *Naka,* the horn. This is carefully watched. It appears in the sky at the beginning of *marega,* winter, the time of drying up. The person who first informs the chief of its being seen, gets a gift from him. When I was young this used to be a great thing, perhaps even a heifer, because Naka signals the end of an old year and the beginning of a new one. On the following day all we diviners gather in the *kgoro* to see what the year will bring.

"Next in importance are *Selemela.*" She waved at the little question mark of the Pleiades. "They tell us when it is time to plough. When they come close to the earth, the grandmothers collect heaps of firewood and when the stars finally sink down, people kindle a fire because that night the cold will begin to strike the trees and leaves will fall.

"Some say that Selemela are the seven virgins who flee from the hunting dog." She brandished her stick at brilliant Sirius, which we too know as the dog star, and Boshier wondered how much the Bantu names owed to Greek mythology, or vice versa.

"The dog chases not only the virgins, but also *Makolobe,* the three wild pigs. See how they run!" She laughed as she traced the file of stars along Orion's belt. Then, suddenly serious, she looked up and along the Milky Way. "When the rocks were still mud and people left their footprints in them, the first children of the great spirit walked along that road toward the rising sun where the lightning bird comes from. Which is why we call it *Molalatladi,* the resting place of the lightning bird. This is your way, too. Walk with care."

He followed the river of stars down to the south and east where it flowed over the edge of the escarpment onto the coastal plains and remembered again his dream of the river that drowned itself in the sea.

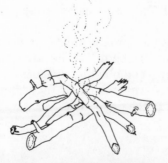

After several months of intensive tuition, Rrasebe decided that Boshier was ready and set the date for his coming out.

"Normally," she said, "the initiation would be held in your home, for that is where your ancestors are. But I will brew the beer here for you and my house will be set apart for this occasion."

The night before the ceremony he was told to abandon his usual blanket and sleep outdoors directly on the earth. "The earth is your mother. Return to her."

In the early morning he came back wearing a white cloth wrapped around his waist. And, in accordance with Rrasebe's instructions, his face was smeared in white clay. In his right hand he carried a small earthen pot containing water collected from the eye of the spring during the night, and in his left a short spear which the modiša had helped him make. He went to the hut in the courtyard, on the door of which was a large white cross, entered, and sat down on a mat at the back.

At sunrise Rrasebe arrived in ceremonial dress, complete with ostrich plumes, sailing through the doorway like a tall ship under full canvas. She fussed over the details in his dress and then they waited together while other dingaka and friends gathered outside in the courtyard. When the time was right, she made a grand exit, stood to one side of the door, and shouted at the top of her considerable voice. "Hrrrrrrrr. Hear me! I have given birth. Look!"

All the visitors broke out clapping and cheering, which was the signal for Boshier to emerge and dance his traditional solo. He put everything he had into it, jumping, stamping, and turning in the traditional way, but adding embellishments owing more to Elvis Presley than African tradition. These were well received, and the way in which he himself set the tempo, rather than simply following the beat of those who were clapping, also caused favorable comment. "He will divine in the way of the spirits," they said, "and not just tell people what they want to hear."

Boshier danced over to the kraal entrance and singled out a large black bull from the herd. This he pointed at with his closed fist, extolling its size and obvious sleekness. There were shouts of admiration from the onlookers, two of whom easily caught the animal and led it to the open area near the kraal.

The novice approached again, this time carrying a single pot of beer which he poured over the animal's shoulders, where the spirits like to sit, and said: "Ye of the Makgabeng. Today I am calling on you. Look at this beast, the one you yourselves have chosen. This is your food today, and the putting out of my fire."

Then he handed his spear to a man who had been pointed out to him as a skilled butcher, indicating that he should stab it in the neck rather than in the traditional spot on its side. Great importance is attached to the noises a sacrificial animal makes as it dies. A quick death without sound is regarded as a failure and an offense to the spirits, so the side spot, although prolonging the agony, is greatly favored. Boshier nevertheless insisted on the neck.

The spear plunged in and the bull sank to its knees, bellowing frightfully. The two men who held the ropes began to pull and push so that it fell properly, on its right side. But the beast threw them off and staggered again to its feet, wild-eyed, with the spear still stuck in its throat and blood gushing from its open mouth. With each rasping breath, it roared and bawled in agony.

The spirits may have been delighted, but Boshier was appalled. He knew the rules. "A diviner must not spill blood. He does not kill." But eventually he could stand it no longer.

The butcher seemed incapable of action, so Boshier leaped forward himself, darting around in front of the horns, and grasped one in his left hand. He leaned forward over it and with his right hand forced the spear deep down in between two of the vertebrae in the animal's neck. It arched once, rising up so that Boshier's feet were lifted clear of the ground, and then it crashed down, stone dead on its right side facing the main hut with the white cross on the door, where Rrasebe stood watching impassively.

The ceremony was completed. The animal was skinned and eaten without salt. The visiting dingaka sang special songs of initiation and the ritual spear was pushed, as is right, through the thatching of the main hut to awaken the spirits living there.

All agreed that the young white novice, who now wore the second shoulder band of a qualified diviner, had been fittingly initiated and would doubtless be someone of power and influence. Still, there was a lingering uneasiness about the slaughter itself. Nobody knew what the consequences of this might be.

There had never been an initiate who killed at his own coming out. Nothing could be done about it now; it was all in the hands of the spirits.

Morara—

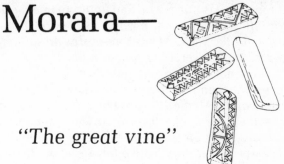

"The great vine"

An essential part of the folklore current among white people in Africa is the story of the witch doctor's pot. The chief's favorite goat, so the story goes, is missing. It is presumed to have been stolen by some passing stranger, until the horns and skin are found hidden in a bush nearby. The culprit is clearly someone in the village itself, someone who succumbed to a craving for fresh meat. But who?

As in all such situations, the resident diviner is consulted. He throws his bones and decides that the best way of establishing guilt is to find an eye-witness. Nobody seems to have actually seen the crime taking place, but there are a number of chickens in a pen nearby. Perhaps one of them has noticed something.

Everybody knows that chickens cannot talk, but the witch doctor assures them that the cockerel, a fine animal with a big red comb, certainly knows the identity of the criminal and can be made to tell by placing it in a large iron cooking pot that stands over the ashes of the chief's last fire.

149

He asks each of the villagers to come up in turn and touch the pot gently, telling them that the bird will be bound to recognize the touch of the guilty party and identify him or her by throwing off the heavy lid and flying up into the air. Everyone in the village files past the pot and puts himself to the test. But even when the last resident has gone by, the lid still remains firmly in place. The cockerel has failed in his duty.

But not the canny witch doctor, who lines everyone up again and then simply goes down the row looking at the palms of their hands. All the villagers have soot-blackened hands except one–the culprit, who, aware of his guilt and afraid of the consequences, only pretended to touch the cooking pot.

It is a good story, with a fine twist, but there are two things wrong with it. The first is that it implies that an African diviner is little more than a trickster, a skilled practical psychologist who relies only on his knowledge of local people and their particular problems in order to ply his trade. The second is the use of the term "witch doctor," with all its unfortunate overtones of evil spells, sorcery, and social turmoil.

The truth is far more magical.

Dramatic ritual is a procedure for grasping the unknown, a way of binding what is grasped into a system of belief. It is a method of incorporating into daily life what is thus grasped and bound. Such a process makes use of all the resources of the culture in which it occurs—everything from instinctive behavior at one end of the scale to language, song, dance, and art at the other. The result is a rich variety of ceremonies that tend to conceal the true concerns, dressing them up in elaborate symbols and disguises, or projecting them onto others in the environment.

Many people do not have our scientific understanding of lightning. If their homes are struck by lighting, it is easier and more acceptable for them to assume that this is the work of a particular moloi, or black magician, than to assume that the planet itself has something personal against them.

A belief in magic makes it easier to account for misfortune, and the existence of appropriate ritual permits people to take action of some sort in the face of uncertainty and insecurity. All this helps to make the occult at least partly manageable. Having identified the source of trouble and having given it a human face, one fights it with magic of one's own, or employs a magician to do so.

There is a choice. Magic has two sides, one "white" and one "black." In general, white magic involves ritual that is open, has collective authorization, and is good. Black magic is secret and antisocial. It is supported by collusion, not consensus, and is bad. Black magic in Africa is practiced by individual moloi, who may be either sorcerers or witches, or more occasionally both.

A sorcerer is one who casts spells against, or puts curses on, others. The acts themselves are usually simple and can theoretically be done by anyone who takes the trouble to collect the necessary materials, or who buys such "medicines" from a specialist. A witch, on the other hand, is someone who has personal power to harm other people directly. Witches, male or female, are thought to be able to travel great distances instantaneously, to use familiars or to turn themselves into animals such as leopards, and to go out in spirit while leaving their bodies asleep at home.

Sorcery is open to investigation by anyone who takes the trouble to find it. Witchcraft is by definition impossible to observe, but belief in its existence is almost universal. In Africa it is a fundamental part of most people's thinking about illness, misfortune, causation, and morality. It is impossible to deal with African society without understanding the role of such beliefs in the lives of people who hold them. It would be simplistic and misleading merely to dismiss these beliefs as products of ignorance and error. A belief in magic is not, after all, so very different from the faith that underpins most religions and provides for secular and social stability. In Africa it has produced an elaborate and sophisticated system of social checks and balances that works as well as most formal constitutions.

Put very simply, it seems to have evolved in this way: The experience of misfortune and the need to account for it produced witches. In societies where they did not exist, they would have had to be invented. And once there were witches and witchcraft, there had to be "witch doctors." The classic "witch doctor" was simply someone who smelled out witches, but such specialists are rare. In practice, all those who detect and combat witchcraft also do other things. They have additional technical and social skills that make the term "witch doctor" misleading and best avoided altogether.

It is difficult to find a term that is not loaded in some way. In most African languages a word implying expertise is used. In Northern Sotho this is "ngaka" and is usually qualified by an adjective which spells out the nature of the expertise more clearly. Potters, blacksmiths, and healers are all "dingaka" because it is recognized that their trades include a strong spiritual element. So too are prophets, priests, rainmakers, mediums, ventriloquists, storytellers, herbalists, and the keepers of tradition.

All these practitioners of the "white" arts and sciences are involved in exploring the occult, in making the unknown accessible to everyday life. It is perhaps most meaningful to describe these experts as "diviners" and to divide them into two broad groups: those who use mechanical aids and those who do not.

Mechanical aids to divination include bones, sticks, shells, leaves, coins, birds, winds, and the pattern of fatty deposits in the mesentery of animal intestines. All these systems are elaborate and carefully codified. Meaning is inherent in the recognized patterns, so there are diviners who go completely by the book. But the best ones are the most sensitive, who allow their interpretations to be influenced by their knowledge of, and intuition about, their clients. Most diviners use mechanical aids as just part of their procedure, as a way of focusing attention on crucial areas.

Those diviners who never use such aids at all are in a minority. They are generally called to their trade by an illness and they too fall into two major categories: those who divine unconsciously in a state of trance or spirit possession, and those who remain fully conscious throughout the session. The latter are rare in Africa and are represented more typically by the traditional Siberian or North American "shaman."

Diviners of all types tend to have some herbal knowledge, though only the herbalist or true "medicine man" specializes in this branch of practical chemistry to the exclusion of everything else. The knowledge and use of herbs in Africa is extensive and impressive. Attempts to collate and catalogue this information are still in their infancy, but the interest taken by major drug companies in such studies attests to the efficacy of many of the traditional cures. Several concoctions tested and now in the process of being analyzed have proved to be effective in the treatment of parasitic and bacterial infection, malaria, tuberculosis, and even some forms of cancer. Oral contraceptives and drugs that induce abortion are known, and several local healers have demonstrated their use of a root infusion as an anesthetic when administered in the form of an enema.

One particularly interesting case on record is that of an elderly man who was admitted to a modern hospital with complications of a compound fracture of the ankle that had become gangrenous and seemed to require amputation. Just before surgery began, a message arrived to tell the man that he was urgently required at home to decide on a matter of inheritance. At the hospital he was warned of the gravity of his situation, but was adamant about leaving.

"It doesn't matter if I die," he said, "as long as I can get back for the family meeting. Otherwise my children will lose all the cattle."

He was sent home by ambulance, but he did not die. Three months later he returned in good health with nothing more than a stiff ankle. He explained that he was treated by a herbalist who prepared a heated mixture of several kinds of herbs and clays. This was poured into a pit dug deep enough to hold the entire leg, until the clay had cooled and hardened. Two men then dragged him out and the cast was wrapped in the leaves of a special palm and left in place for six weeks.

The main principles of orthopedic surgery were involved: antiseptics had been used; traction and accurate immobilization had been applied; and the result was dramatic—a complete cure. The best remedy that modern medicine had offered was to cut off the offending part.

Whether or not he or she is involved in healing, a diviner's prime function is to grasp consciously, and to bring out into the open, the secret and unconscious motives causing an individual to become ill, or creating a social disturbance.

Diviners are, in effect, the psychologists, psychiatrists, physicians, priests, confessors, counselors, and historians of their people. All these functions are wrapped up in a single and *highly effective institution. A sympathetic study of the ways in which they work provides valuable insights into the origins not only of magical belief, but of all religion.*

Soon after his own initiation as a "first pot" diviner, the lowest level of such office, Adrian Boshier was given two vivid demonstrations of the talents of other practitioners.

On one occasion he had been asked to help the manager of a large department store find a pistol stolen from his office during a brief absence. Police in Africa deal harshly with those who lose weapons and the man was more anxious to get his gun back than to find or prosecute the thief, who he thought to be one of his own black staff.

A diviner seemed the best answer, so Boshier took one he had just met along to the store. She was a tiny woman, barely five feet tall, but, decked out in beads and red ochre, she carried all the authority of her profession. In the store she caused some consternation by going directly into possession-trance on the showroom floor, screaming in a high-pitched voice and writhing on the ground.

She emerged triumphant from this session with her spirit to announce that the missing object was "a gun that is held in the hand." (In accordance with accepted practice with diviners, she had been told only that something was missing and given no insulting details.) She looked very hard at one of the male assistants and then announced that the weapon was hidden in a toilet, and suggested that she and Boshier go to fetch it. She led him straight out the staff door of the store into a courtyard, opened the door of a lavatory, and pointed at an old-fashioned water cistern high up on the wall. Boshier climbed up on the seat, unbolted the lid of the cistern, put his arm into the tank, and found that his hand closed almost immediately over a loaded automatic pistol. This was returned without further ado to its flabbergasted but extremely grateful owner.

Part of the traditional training undergone by all novice diviners is a game involving "smelling out" or finding hidden objects. At the beginning of their training, the novices are given clues by their teachers and told what to look for and when they are getting "warm"; but toward the end of their apprenticeship, each is expected to operate totally without overt guidance.

Boshier himself tested a diviner on one occasion, hiding the cured skin of a gemsbok antelope beneath a tarpaulin in the back of a vehicle parked a hundred yards away—before even suggesting to her that he had a test in mind. The diviner readily accepted the challenge and began to go into trance. She sighed and belched, yawned and moaned, continually mopping her brow and fanning herself with a spirit broom. Finally, the dam of conscious control broke and she fell to her knees, alternately roaring in a deep, bass growl or producing an earsplitting, high-pitched trill. She rose once more to her feet and started the heel-stamping dance of a diviner, building up to a faster and faster tempo as she began to sing her spirit song. At first her words were raspy and barely audible, but soon they strengthened until they poured out in a constant verbal stream.

"It is large. Made by God. It is very large. It is colored, many-colored. An animal. Part of an animal. Above the ground. Hidden. On wheels. East. Over there. Over there!"

Suddenly she began to run around the building to where the vehicle was parked. She went right up to the truck and pulled open the door of the cab. Finding it empty, she backed away in confusion. Then she knelt and, tearing a string of blue glass beads from her throat, held them out in front of her like a divining rod. For a moment she remained there, motionless, and then without further hesitation, rose, climbed onto the back of the truck, and threw back a blue canvas sailcloth which lay there. Beneath it was the antelope skin, which by custom now belonged to her.

These diviners were able, apparently without prompting or access to any visual cues, to determine not only the nature of the object sought, but its exact location. We call this clairvoyance or telepathy, but in any language it is an impressive, albeit uncontrolled, demonstration of paranormal ability. It would be wrong,

however, to try to isolate such ability for scientific analysis. It would almost certainly prove to be no more fruitful in producing answers than similar talents in our culture have been when subject to laboratory investigation. The reality they represent is too fragile to withstand that kind of scrutiny.

Adrian Boshier realized that the true importance and significance of these abilities, whether they were real or not, lay in their social and environmental context, where they could be seen to be full of meaning. African society is a community of survivors and spirits. Neither can exist without the other, and everything is arranged to emphasize and strengthen this interdependence. Those still alive vitalize the spirits with their memories and prayers, while those who have died mediate and keep a watchful eye on their descendents.

One of the most important powers attributed to spirits is their ability to "see," to provide information about matters removed from ordinary perception.

Unlike Boshier, most anthropologists approach a study of this subject with the premise that the practitioner does not do what he or she claims to do—that a diviner does not, in fact, divine. Reasoning from this assumption, they suggest that diviners are peripheral forces in society, likely to do as much harm as good.

Boshier discovered for himself that divination works extraordinarily well. It functions first at a personal level, relieving doubt and anxiety. Divination is always associated with a situation that seems to call for a decision that cannot easily be taken. For each society there is a proper list of such occasions, which may include illness, death, marriage, calamity, loss, or merely unresolved conflict. Recourse to a diviner, whether the advice is good or bad, true or false, relieves these tensions and provides the psychological release which comes from conviction that a decision is in tune with the wishes of supernatural forces—in other words, that it has the blessing of the spirits.

The diviner, however, is not just a sort of primitive therapist; divination also has important social consequences. It may, for instance, be used to decide where to build a new house. The choice of a site will determine to a very large extent where a particular family is to be placed in social space. It highlights the nature of their relationship with all those around them, and can scarcely be regarded as a decision affecting the head of that house alone.

Most techniques used in divination involve simple mechanical procedures, such as throwing bones, shells, or sticks, or reading the pattern in the entrails of a sacrificial animal. As such, they would seem to be random devices, taking decisions out of the realm of human agency, but they still depend on social consensus.

The actions of even a chief are subject to omens. No traditional ruler in Africa ever acted according to his judgment alone, without the possibility of interference by others, most notably by his diviners. But even the interpretation of the diviners is conditioned by social factors. It has to be couched in terms that are understandable and acceptable to the society as a whole, who thus become the ultimate arbiters. It is less important, therefore, to know how, or even if, a system of divination works, and more useful to understand how it is supposed to work. To be valuable in an individual situation, or valid in a social context, a diviner and a technique of divination need only have dramatic truth. They must be appropriate.

In a small settlement, deep in a valley of the Makgabeng, lived a terrified man named Phuti.

Phuti was cursed.

It came about as a result of an argument over the offspring of a particular cow, but it soon became a feud that set two entire families against each other. In the end one of the families had employed the services of a moloi, skilled in the casting of spells. They had chosen Rakumaku, a lean, yellowish man with the most evil reputation in the mountains.

Rakumaku called down lightning on Phuti's village and a week later a bolt hit the goat kraal and killed every animal in it. He did it again and before long the cattle kraal was hit, with similar consequences. Then he promised to bring about a third strike that would kill the entire family.

A year had passed and this final prophecy had not yet been fulfilled, but Phuti and his wives and children lived in constant fear. Such was the reputation of the moloi that nobody cared to set himself up against him publicly in a trial of strength. Rrasebe had quietly worked a few things of her own, but they had not helped. Good magic should be done in the open, in front of all the people, to be truly effective; only witchcraft and sorcery flourish in the dark.

Adrian Boshier knew Phuti well. The stricken man walked often in the mountains and had helped Boshier find several interesting caves. He decided, in return, to see what he could do about getting the curse lifted. He realized that his best chance lay in dramatics and looked, accordingly, for a suitable snake. As always, he had no trouble finding one.

As Boshier and Phuti approached a spring near the foot of the cursed valley, a herdboy came running toward them chattering about two huge snakes that had commandeered the only local source of water. The child led them to a reed-covered area which had been partly trampled by thirsty cattle, and Boshier went ahead alone and made a slow, careful circuit of the eye of the spring.

This revealed nothing, so he made two more sweeps, one closer to the pool and another further out. It seemed as though the snakes had gone, so Phuti and the boy came closer. In the meantime, Boshier continued to poke around in the thicker clumps of reed with his stick.

Suddenly two things happened at once. Boshier felt a

thump against the side of his knee and heard two terrified yells as his companions bolted out of the reeds and disappeared into the bush. He looked down and found a huge yellowish Egyptian cobra right there beside him, struggling to rear itself up and deliver another attack. He pinned the snake down with his stick, grasped it around the neck, and picked it up. Then he examined his leg and found that, somehow, the cobra's fangs had not even broken the skin.

The snake was almost eight feet long and fatter than any of its species he had ever seen. He carried it out of the reeds and laid it down again on a patch of open ground, where it lay still for a few minutes. Then the reason for its lethargy, its exceptional girth, and its inability to bite properly all became clear. It promptly regurgitated a second snake, another cobra of the same species, but a little shorter. Boshier's would-be killer was a cannibal.

He picked it up again just as Phuti came rushing back reinforced by several men from a nearby village. They were incredulous to find Boshier playing with the snake, apparently unharmed. Boshier tried to explain that it had not actually bitten him, whereupon the men turned on Phuti and demanded a detailed explanation. The man gave a graphic description of the snake rearing up with hood spread and striking Boshier's leg. Then everyone had to examine and marvel over his unblemished right knee. The consensus was simple. Rradinoga had done it again. The "father of snakes" had once more demonstrated the power he had over his "children."

Armed with a snake that was to become a legend in the mountains, he had what he needed to stage an exorcism, but he covered all bets by practicing a little of the herbal lore he had acquired during his training. From a dry northern slope he took a gross, fleshy corkwood shrub known locally as "cannot die," because it seems to be able to survive frost, fire, pestilence, and even a direct strike by lightning. This he crushed and mixed with bark, roots, and leaves from every other plant known to have any connection at all with thunder or lightning. He pressed the whole blend into the shell of a giant snail. Then he told Phuti to let the word be put about that the curse on his home would be lifted the following morning.

A large crowd turned up to watch. Boshier waited until the moment was right and then stepped out of Phuti's hut with a flourish, wearing his beaded headband with its goat gall bladder ornament. He had draped a bright red cloth across his shoulders, "because a diviner ceases to dream if these parts are exposed to the sun." In his left hand he carried the snail shell with its lightning repellent medicine and in his right a spirit broom. As he crossed the courtyard he began aloud to call on all his ancestors by name, asking them to rally round him and the unfortunate Phuti.

"Remember," said Rrasebe, "the people believe in evil because evil exists. There is evil as sure as there is goodness. The power of the moloi is real and can even kill. Only a fool would disregard this. Only someone with greater power, and the help of the people, can fight it."

Boshier crossed to the gateway and, with a dramatic flourish, whipped away a skin covering one of the pillars that stood on either side of the entrance. Beneath it lay the bright painting of a double-headed creature, the traditional preventer-of-evil, which he had drawn there by moonlight the previous night. There was a murmur of approval from the crowd, but this quickly turned to a ripple of amusement when a voice from the far side of the enclosure asked loudly, "Who is this woman whom Phuti has employed to paint his house?"

It was Rakumaku, who leaned arrogantly on the courtyard wall, a sneer on his yellow face. "Does she think she will be paid for her work? Why does she not look around this poor village and ask herself where are all the goats and cattle?"

Boshier ignored him and went on with the ritual, annointing each of the structures in the yard with his herbal brew. He began to dance and Phuti joined him, carrying a pure white cockerel.

"Watch out the chicken doesn't eat you!" Rakumaku was getting too much response from the crowd at their expense.

The chicken was swiftly beheaded, cut open, and Phuti unhesitatingly swallowed its gall bladder while Boshier scattered blood around the doorway to each of the huts. When the preparations were complete, he went to squat in the very center of the yard in front of a large clay pot with a stone lid. But the

moloi continued to hold the crowd's attention with an elaborate
pantomime centered on a dark cloud overhead. He pretended to
feel a drop of rain and began to search the sky for signs of
lighting.

It was time for the finale. Boshier reached out and knocked
the lid from the pot. He hit the side twice with his fly whisk and,
right on cue, the cobra rose up to its full impressive height and
stood there with hood spread, swaying and peering short-
sightedly at the crowd. There was a gasp from the onlookers and
several screams as a movement caught the snake's attention and
it swung round to face in that direction. Rakumaku was forgotten.

Distracting the reptile with his switch, Boshier reached out
and grabbed it by the neck, pulling all the snake out of the pot.
He held its whole enormous length aloft, writhing in both hands
over his head, as he turned toward the mountains and called
loudly on the Great Serpent to recognize its child.

Boshier lowered the snake slowly and worked his fingers
into a position where it was possible to force its mouth open to
show the white gleam of its fangs. He squeezed the glands at the
back of the cobra's head and two streams of yellowish venom
flowed out into his cupped left hand. Then Adrian Boshier did a
terrible thing: he drank it.

Snake venom is a specialized form of saliva. Drops of it
inevitably find their way into the reptile's own throat and
stomach, where the toxic proteins are safely digested before they
can enter the bloodstream. A healthy human can deal with the
poison in precisely the same way. Unless there are internal cuts
or ulcers or cavities in the teeth, drinking venom is quite safe—
even though it is not a pleasant sight to watch.

Even Rakumaku was impressed by this feat. He watched
silently as Boshier walked around the bounds of the courtyard,
spitting dramatically at each corner, building up a barrier of
venom to protect the village. Then, holding the snake up with its
jaws agape and fangs still dripping, Boshier turned and walked
directly toward the moloi.

Rakumaku stood his ground. He twitched a little and turned
a shade paler, but he remained rooted to the spot, staring in
horrid fascination at the snake Boshier held up only inches from
his face. The crowd was completely silent and the air was stiff

with tension as the impasse grew. The moloi would not back down and Boshier knew that he could not actually let the snake bite the man.

In the end the snake itself resolved the situation by emitting an awful, low, hollow hiss. The sound jerked Rakumaku back into full terrified consciousness. He made a small childlike sound in his throat, turned, and fled. The tension broke as the people roared their approval. Without a word to anyone, Boshier quietly took his snake and left.

Phuti had been cursed, which of course made him uncomfortable. The subsequent lightning strikes reinforced his belief in the power of the moloi and effectively destroyed hope for his life. Even if there was no connection between the curse and its fulfillment, it worked because Phuti let it do so. The people of the village were intimately involved in all this. Their attitude toward what had taken place confirmed his diagnosis and endorsed their joint belief in the efficacy of magic. Rakumaku, whatever his talent, must have been equally impressed, so he too was involved in the consensus. The whole community was locked into a set of assumptions that virtually condemned Phuti to death.

Had there been only one lightning strike, Rrasebe or some other ngaka might have succeeded in working rival magic to counteract the curse. But the second strike put the situation beyond normal social controls. An outside force was needed to set the balance in motion again. Adrian Boshier provided the necessary impetus. What he did was sufficiently traditional to give it credence. He used enough of the local vocabulary of belief to enable it to work; and because he was an outsider as well as an initiate, he was free to improvise in ways which would have been unacceptable for a homegrown diviner.

Rakumaku was defeated, not just to Phuti's satisfaction, but in front of the people. He did not have to be forced to withdraw the curse. His public humiliation was sufficient for a tacit agreement to be reached on the matter. Nobody ever mentioned it again. Within two years Phuti had built up his herds once more and was a normal, prosperous member of the community.

Temoso—

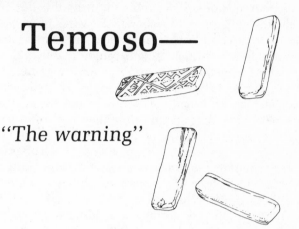

"The warning"

Adrian Boshier never came near to realizing the tribal efficiency of a true diviner, but given the constraints of his particular personality and the brevity of his life, he did astonishingly well.

His snakes helped, by providing him with ready-made symbols of great power. These are exactly the sort of "tools" a good diviner needs. Boshier was able in certain situations to use this material wisely in ways that helped to redress social imbalances and assist others to adjust to the cultural shock that is a routine part of black-white relationships in Africa. But he had trouble making it work for himself.

The epilepsy that gave him access to other realities and to the secrets of tradition also provided a continuing trauma that put him at odds with those around him. He was never completely comfortable in his skin. No one understood this better than Rrasebe. On one occasion she took him to see a nest of communal spiders.

In the bushveld there are many lace or mesh-web spiders.

Individually they are small and insignificant, but together they build substantial nests—tough opaque structures several inches across, made of twigs, leaves, and dust held together by closely woven strands of silk. Running out from this den in all directions, the spiders build elaborate networks of web designed to exploit local conditions to advantage and snare as many insects as possible. When something is caught in one of their nets, the tiny short-legged spiders converge on it together. There is no hurry, no rush to bite. They move in slowly from every direction with purposeful intent and gather round the captive, waiting apparently for some signal before they settle down next to one another on the quivering body and all bite at the same time.

"We are like *segoko*," Rrasebe said. "Each of us is small and of little importance, but we are part of something far bigger. Together we belong to a system which has much power. From tiny threads we build a great vine, and make of it a place for catching evil. But just seeing and holding evil is not enough; we need to destroy it. We cannot do that unless we work together, and we cannot work as one unless there is a signal. Unless one among us beats the drum. That is our duty as dingaka.

"I have tried to teach you the way of this thing. You have learned well and I believe you understand. You are strong, but there is a wildness about you that makes you walk alone. You dance to a different drum and bite the evil all on your own. So far you have been lucky and have survived, but sooner or later it will bite back.

"You cannot fight it alone. You must let the spirits help you, instead of fighting them as well. To work, they need light. I have given you an eye, but it is still closed and there is darkness inside."

She tapped him gently on the forehead with her spirit broom.

"The spirits are angry and the sickness is their sign. Give them what they need. Let them feed alongside you."

He heard and he understood, but it frightened him in ways that charging elephants and angry mambas had never been able to do.

Once again he fled from the Makgabeng, returning to the more mundane, more predictable, and less personally threatening world of life in a big city.

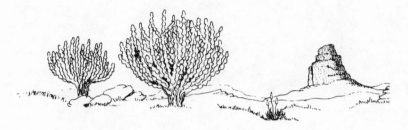

Part Four

"The earth is like the breasts of a woman,
useful as well as pleasing."

Sotho proverb.

EARTH

The first European explorers entered the interior of Africa at the beginning of the last century. They found flourishing Bantu communities living there in much the same way as the people still do in rural areas today. But they also found evidence of another kind of civilization, characterized by ancient mines, elaborate terraces, and decorated stone walls, many of them already in ruins.

The tendency at that time, one which is still current in some official circles today, was to assume that the indigenous people of Africa could never have built such sophisticated structures. They were seen as evidence for the existence in sub-Saharan Africa of a pre-Bantu civilization, and used by a number of writers to further their own theories about the Queen of Sheba, Hiram King of Tyre, and the Lost Tribes of Israel. A group of the most spectacular monuments at Zimbabwe were made famous by Rider Haggard in King Solomon's Mines. And since his time, a number of others have looked for similar connections with Egypt, Crete, or the Middle East.

These romantic notions were attacked in the 1920s by the formidable Gertrude Caton-Thompson, a British archaeologist who has left a lasting mark on African studies. Tall and white-haired, dressed always in a gray flannel tailored suit with a matching felt hat, she traveled and excavated indefatigably, looking always as cool and composed as if she were attending a vicar's tea party. Ms. Caton-Thompson insisted that the ruins at Zimbabwe, and others like them, were of no great antiquity and must be attributed totally to a local culture. She dismissed the Oriental pottery and Arabian beads as evidence merely of much later trade with the powerful African chiefs who had built and lived in these strongholds in medieval times.

The majority of archaeological opinion today goes along with her conclusions, seeing the builders in stone as the southern end of a disconnected series of communities spread from the Sudan all the way to the Cape. There are certainly modern groups who still exercise some of the ancient skills. The Southern Sotho, who now live mainly in the Kingdom of Lesotho, are skilled masons, building elaborate stone walls without the use of mortar.

There would seem on the surface of it to be no persistent puzzle about the origin of the stone ruins. But there are still a number of disturbing and unanswered questions. Many of these, of course, are being asked by Raymond Dart, one of the few who ever dared cross swords with the redoubtable Gertrude.

"It is my contention," he says, "that archaeologists have failed to assess these ruins in relation to their total setting. They must be seen as part of a cultural complex which takes full account of ancient mining, of terraced irrigation, and of seaborne contacts with people foreign to Africa."

There are certainly some fascinating loose ends. In 1901 a German archaeologist discovered a pottery figurine on the Zambezi River close to Umtali. A description of his find was published in a German journal and was later the subject of correspondence in the Times of London with noted British Egyptologist Sir Flinders Petrie. The statue was sent to Petrie who identified it as "an Ushabte figure of moulded clay with the cartouche of Tahutmes III (about 1450 B.C.) on its chest. On the head is an elaborate wig, in each hand a scourge and below the

waist three lines of inscription so effaced that only the title
Osiris can be seen. The figure is certainly genuinely ancient and
has long been buried in moist earth."

There seems to be no mention of the find in any other
literature since 1906. But it is worth recording that the name
given in ancient Egyptian records for an almost mythical sacred
land far to the south, inhabited by the Shades (Bantu) and
Dwarfs (San), was Punt. In Egyptian, "p" and "b" are not clearly
distinguished. It is highly likely that Punt stands for Bunt(u), the
land of the people, the ones who call themselves Bantu.

In 1963, a Swazi man digging a sand pit on the banks of the
Umbeluzi River near Mlaula came across the head and body of a
crystalline limestone statue. Such rock is foreign to the area and
the figure is clearly not African. It shows a smooth, rounded face
with almond eyes and hair tied into a topknot. The torso is
dressed only in a loincloth.

An expert from the Department of Oriental Antiquities at
the British Museum later identified it as Bengali and as "a
representation of the god Krishna. Were it completed, it could
show him standing with ankles crossed and playing the flute." It
has never been dated and no adequate explanation has yet been
advanced for its discovery, many feet underground, at a point
over fifty miles inland from the nearest possible seaport.

There are many such intrusive oddities tucked away in
African collections, most of them conveniently swept under the
rug of current orthodoxy.

The current myth about Africa, prompted perhaps by growing nationalism, stresses the strength, vitality, and indepen-
dence of indigenous influences. This is a valid and worthy
emphasis, long overdue in academic disciplines that have
tended to belittle African culture. But it ought not to conceal the
very real probability that the Bantu civilizations who worked
the mines and built Zimbabwe may have been influenced by,
and in turn have influenced, visitors who came right into Africa
long before the first Dutch or Portuguese rounded the Cape.

Another possibility is that these visitors might have been
exploring, mining, and trading on the continent with its original
KhoiSan inhabitants long before the majority of Bantu came
south with the new agricultural revolution. It is surely signifi-

cant that both the Egyptian and Indian statues were found on major rivers, which would have been logical routes through the escarpment onto the plateau of the interior. A new and much more revolutionary idea is that the KhoiSan themselves, the first Africans, started the whole thing.

There has been an unfortunate tendency in African archaeology to assume that culture and race go necessarily hand in hand—that Bantu skeletons must be connected with agriculture; that KhoiSan remains can never be so associated; that mining is an activity for settled and therefore Bantu or foreign communities; and that mining can have played no part in the lives of the nomadic KhoiSan.

These assumptions have led to a sharp distinction between the Stone Age and the Iron Age, as though the terms and the cultures were mutually exclusive. The true picture is far more complex, and much more interesting.

Iron is not an easy metal to work. Copper and gold have much lower melting points and are more simply handled. Copper is easier to smelt and gold is generally found in a metallic state which needs no melting at all. In most parts of the world, therefore, these relatively soft metals appear in the chronology long before iron, whose production required a far more elaborate technology.

This sequence, however, conceals the fact that iron ore occurs in a number of forms, some of which were sought not for their hardness, but for their visual qualities. Beginning five thousand years ago, the so-called Iron Age swept through the world, changing lives with its myths, rites, and metallurgical mysteries. But there is now good evidence to show that more than forty thousand years before Bantu arrived in southern Africa with their pottery and hand-blown forges, iron ore was already being mined there by people with stone tools.

Blood-red hematite and glistening specularite were being excavated deep underground in Africa at a time when Europe was still inhabited by Neanderthal Man.

Metal was beginning to work its strange magic on our minds. In Africa it seems to have given rise to symbolism, ritual, ideology, language, and the birth of human consciousness.

Lefoka—

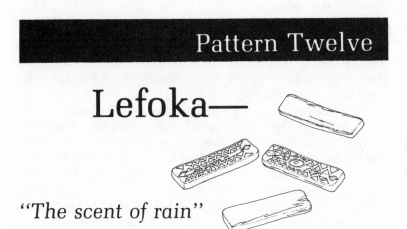

"The scent of rain"

It was a time of drought. For miles around the grass had shriveled and died. The rivers were dry and the cattle had become scrawny. There was little point in moving them from the kraals where they stood listlessly, heads hung low, for there was no grazing to be found anywhere in the Makgabeng.

Adrian Boshier had not been back to the mountains for several years, and he was shocked and saddened by the ravages wrought by the lack of rain—and by the changes in the people. He, too, had changed. He had immersed himself in the work of the Museum of Man and Science, running field trips, mounting exhibitions, making films, and giving lectures. He had organized a research project designed to explore the origin, training, and talents of spirit-diviners, using his status as an initiate to attract others to the work. But he had gone no further with his own training, and now the epileptic attacks had begun again in earnest.

For two years after he killed the bull, he had not felt a single

175

epileptic sensation, but now he was being struck down roughly once a month, with increasing severity. He had, in fact, come back to the Makgabeng to talk with Rrasebe about going on to the next step in his training.

For the first time in his association with the mountains, he came in a four-wheel-drive vehicle. On his arrival, he had gone to sleep in a hut vacated for him by one of the blind chief's wives. He awoke a few hours later to find the village almost deserted.

Among the few signs of life was an old woman who sat on the ground across the courtyard in the sun working on a leather garment. The women sit with their legs straight out in front of them, backs stiff, never leaning against a wall or tree, because to do so would be seen as a sign of laziness.

The old woman smiled cheerfully and waved at him. Boshier went over. "Dumela, mother."

"Dumela," she agreed. "*Lekae,* how are you?"

"*Regona,*" he replied, "still alive." She smiled again and watched him with her watery old eyes.

"The village is quiet," he said. "Where are all the people?"

"Out," she waved toward the fields at the foot of the cliffs, "cleansing the land."

He had heard the expression go *hlatswa* before and knew that it had something to do with the rainmaking ritual. It was October, the month of the moon that bursts, when the Southern Cross sets just before bedtime, but the rains had not yet come.

"And you, mother?"

"I am *bollo,* my son. Hot, because my husband is but recently dead. Our blood was one, and now he is gone, I burn for him and my feet scorch the ground. I remain here until the cure is complete, lest I injure others and keep away the rain."

He walked through the village toward the lands, noticing as he passed the well that the water was very low and badly fouled. A crowd of people, most of the adult villagers, were gathered around a cairn of stone, facing away from it, looking away across the plain. He joined them and at first could see nothing. Then he heard the sound of high-pitched voices singing in the distance. A large group of girls wearing only tiny aprons front and back came into view, winding up through the dry fields, each carrying a small clay pot and a bunch of twigs like a broom.

Where will the cattle drink?
Let it rain, let it rain.
And the white-breasted crow?
Let it rain, let it rain.
Don't you see the land is scorched?
Let us live by the water of your rain.

As they sang, the girls used their brooms to sprinkle sacred water on the edges of the land, cleansing it and summoning the clouds.

When the throng got closer, the people fell back and the girls approached the cairn. Each in turn poured what was left of the liquid in her pot onto the mound, where it trickled down and was soon swallowed up by the parched sand.

Then a man with a red cloth draped across his shoulders stepped forward and placed on the ground an antelope horn plugged with grass. This was *moroka pula*, the rain doctor, who said:

I speak about rain,
Soft steady rain.
Let the eland die,
Let the fountains run.
Pull the clouds together,
Let it rain.

The people waved their arms above their heads and shouted in the voice of people everywhere, "*Agone pula*, let it rain!"

Rain is the elixir of life.

Almost everywhere in Africa rain is the determining factor between sufficiency and want. Never far from the people's thoughts, rain is a subject of daily conversation. One of the most polite ways of thanking a person is to say, "I make it rain for you." And to someone who leaves it is said, "Go with rain," or "Come back with rain." A child born in a good year may be called "One-who-comes-with-rain." And another in a bad year, "One-who-comes-from-waterless-valley."

The people recognize that "smoke is fire, but clouds are not necessarily rain." And that "rain is a stranger who has his own home." But they believe that "rain never dies up above," that it can be summoned by the appropriate ritual, or discouraged by a failure to observe all the necessary taboos.

In the season of rain it is necessary to build a special rain kraal or "rain yard," and to organize hunting expeditions for the dung of pela, the rock hyrax, and the flesh of kololo, the klip-springer. These are used in the preparation of the medicines of the rain pots, which are taken out for cleansing the land or pegging the boundaries. And it is here in the kraal that a great fire is lit in order that its smoke "may summon up the clouds."

In the case of severe drought it is thought to be necessary to slaughter an ox or bull (which needs to be black "because the rain clouds are dark") and spread its entrails over the graves of former chiefs. During the whole of the growing period, when rains are most crucial, it is forbidden to plough, clear new land, cut grass for thatching, castrate young bulls, or drink water while standing up. Such acts are believed to "drive away the rain." In addition, it is inadvisable to kill lizards or crocodiles, to dig pot clay, to lean pestles together against a wall, or to touch a tree in which the lightning bird has settled.

Recently widowed women, or those who have had a miscarriage, are said to be "hot" and in need of cooling down. Their relatives bring them special medicines and they are obliged to remain at home until the process is complete or "the country will be spoiled and no rain will come." If a woman should give birth or a man should die in the lands, or the fields should happen to be struck by lightning, they must be purified again by sprinkling them with special rain medicines. And because drought is one of the greatest punishments brought down on humanity by its transgressions, it may even be necessary to kill one or both of a pair of unfortunate twins.

In many instances such ceremony is presided over by a special rainmaker or rain doctor, but ultimately rain is the responsibility of the chief. It is he who must intercede with the ancestors when "the people are crying." It is he who can constrain the heavens, transform clouds, raise storms, and send hurricanes. He is the one with power to withhold rain from the undeserving or, with mechanical precision, to drop it gently on the faithful.

He is beseeched by the people in their kiba dance, a slow stately rhythm done to the accompaniment of just two drums. It is begun in the dim light of dawn and only those who have lost at least one parent may perform. As they stamp and turn all day, the dust rises high and by sunset everyone is covered by sweat and dirt. But next day and the next they come again, hoping to touch the heart of the chief and evoke his pity at the sorrowful sight of people dancing in the summer when they ought to be ploughing. And when, despite everything, the rains fail, it is at the chief's kraal that the women gather dressed in rags, with their breasts uncovered, each carrying a long unstripped cane. They set about him with their sticks and then take over his kgotla, singing and dancing in anger, wearing down its surface and thrashing every man who comes within reach.

When it does rain, there is great rejoicing. The omens are good and as the people pass each other in the fields they raise their arms high and shout, "Pula. Pula. Pula! Rain. Rain. Rain!"

The old chief was blind, and the people wondered whether this might not have something to do with the drought.

"He no longer has rain in his hands," they said. "And the only clouds to be seen are the ones that cover his eyes."

Late one afternoon an assembly was called in the village kgoro for the purpose of "discussing the rain." The chief was carried out to his place and the council of elders formed itself around him. When everyone was in position, the head councillor said, "We seek rain from you, chief." And the old man replied, "I hear you; and the rain will fall."

But this was clearly only a ritual opening, because the discussion then began on what could be done about the drought. To his consternation, Adrian Boshier found that they turned soon to where he sat at the end of the line on the chief's right-hand side.

"What would you demand," asked an elder, "to make the rain walk again through our land?"

Boshier protested that he was not a rain doctor.

"Yes, we know this, but you could do it nevertheless. We would pay you well."

He tried again to say that he knew nothing of rainmaking, but the same man cut him short. "Are you not Rradinoga?"

He admitted that he was, at which the whole council nodded at each other as though this was proof of his ability. He tried to change the subject by suggesting tentatively that they might pray for rain.

The old blind chief snapped, "That would be a waste of time. Modimo is indeed the master, the supreme being, and there are those who can talk directly with him. He is like a lion who is in charge, but it is the lion's wives, not he, who bring down the food. The missionaries tell us that God does everything himself, but that is obviously ridiculous. Whoever heard of a chief that did all the work? The chief has his people, the lion has his wives, and God has his servants, seriti, the spirits. It is they we must approach.

"That is why we are asking you to help us. To work in the way you have been shown by the spirits. You never offered us rules like the missionaries. Instead you walked always with the spirits, who looked after you where others would have died. You catch and talk to the spirits. We have seen you doing this. We believe that this drought may be upon us because one of the shades, perhaps the Great Serpent himself, has been offended. You, with your snakes, are obviously the one to make amends."

He tried desperately to find some way of explaining that he was young and inexperienced and . . .

"Where were you born?" asked the chief.

"In England," he replied.

The old man looked pleased. "That is good. It is known that Leisimane, the Englishmen, are born next to God. Furthermore, the king of England is one hundred and fifty years old, even though I am told he looks still like a young man. Now it is clear why you come to us with so much power for one so young. You are just like King George!"

There was nothing Boshier could say. To have told them that England was now ruled by a woman would only have caused confusion. (For all he knew, they might have been referring to George the Third or Fourth!)

"Why have you returned to us now?" asked an elder. "Is there some special reason? Did not the spirits send you?"

Boshier explained that he had come to see Rrasebe about his health.

"Is it the falling sickness?" asked the chief. "The illness of the apprentice which we experienced with you?"

He admitted that it was and they all exchanged knowing looks. It *was* the spirits who had sent him.

The old chief strained upright in his chair. "Will you help us? Will you go once more into the mountains and speak with the spirits? Will you tell them that the people are being killed and need rain?"

He realized that this was the least he could do. "I will go tonight."

The old chief beckoned to him to come closer, and when he did, grasped his wrist with an old gnarled hand. "Take this," he said, holding out his stick with the other hand. "I carved it with my own hands. May you use it to walk well, unhindered by all. And may your path soon lead you back. Come back with rain."

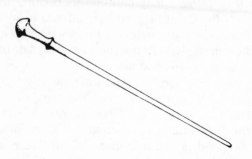

It was dark by the time Boshier walked out of the village and entered the gorge beyond. But it was cool, and there were no flies. The moon was bright enough to throw the floor of the ravine into sharp relief and make it easy for him to pick his way through the maze of rock. He was familiar with this territory and so continued until he reached the high plateau. The area on top was flat, but sprinkled with boulders and great slabs of stone to form a warren of shelters and passageways, some so narrow that he had to squeeze to get through.

Wandering among those rock formations in the moonlight

was like exploring some vast ghost city. It was easy to imagine the eyes of the inhabitants following his every movement. At one point a nightjar (whippoorwill) burst up off the ground at his feet, startling him, and the feeling of being watched became so strong that he whirled round to look back. What he saw was not human, but it brought the illusion of the city completely to life because it was undoubtedly man-made. Thrown across a gap between two giant boulders, and winding over to enclose several overhangs and shelters, was the most beautiful wall he had ever seen.

The smooth stones stood stark and clean in the moonlight, the cracks between them thin black lines too fine to take the blade of a knife. He followed the line of the wall down to a deep dry shelter, which felt so right that he unrolled his blanket and soon fell asleep, there alone in his own lost city.

For days Boshier lived there in seclusion, sharing the ruins with small, shy duiker antelope and a large troop of baboon. The latter showed little fear and allowed him to approach quite close, but when he overstepped an invisible boundary line a big male would stand and bark at him defiantly, setting off a chorus of calls among the others.

During the days he wandered among the old cliff dwellings, climbing endlessly and employing every survival trick learned in the early years. It was even harder now in this time of drought, but he managed and it gave him great satisfaction to be there and to succeed. Every night he slept in a different cave. He found that many of the deeper ones had been subdivided by stone walls and a few still showed signs of paving. Scattered everywhere in the dust were stone tools, potsherds and, once in a while, a glass trade bead.

Each day was filled with the simple thrill of exploration; each night was punctuated by the yelps of distant jackal or the cultured conversation of a pair of resident eagle owl.

Boshier began to feel very close to the spirits. He was half convinced that they were there, that they had summoned him, and that there was something he could do. On the seventh day he found it.

At first it looked like nothing more than a cleft in the rock wall about fifteen feet above the valley floor. But when he climbed up to it, he found that it soon opened out into a sizeable cave illuminated by a shaft of light from a second entrance high up at the back of the cavern.

It was a treasure house. Half buried in dust and debris on one side were four large clay storage pots. Two were shattered but the others were intact and in one was the shell of a giant land snail containing four tortoise leg bones of the sort he had seen among the bones of other diviners. Nearby were the partially burned skull of a large giraffe and a spiral kudu horn, but on a rock shelf at the other side of the cave was the greatest prize.

Lying in a pile, like pencils fallen from a jar, were a number of short, worn sticks with smooth rounded ends: drumsticks. And beside them, stacked neatly beneath the overhang, a set of five superb wooden drums. They were pot-shaped and carved, handles and all, each from a single solid block of wood. On the large ones, perhaps two feet in diameter, the handles took the form of crossed struts; the smaller ones bore one or two simple cylindrical knobs. Two of the drums were decorated with raised tooth patterns on the side and all had been pierced around the rim with a hot iron to allow an antelope-skin drumhead to be stretched across the open mouth and anchored with a number of short wooden pegs.

They were clearly very old, for the wood had begun to split and rot, and on two of them the skin had perished completely through. Boshier stood and gaped. The drums were covered with dust but the whole arrangement was so deliberate, so clearly theatrical, that it reminded him of the carefully contrived informality common to displays in many modern collections. He had seen drums of this quality before, but only in a museum. There was, however, something very special, almost magical, about these.

It was not just that he had found them himself. There was a delicacy, an air of reverence, about the way in which they had been placed. It was as though the last person to touch them had handled each with loving care and put them down just so, knowing that he would never see them again, and hoping whoever did, would recognize and respect them for what they were.

Adrian Boshier knew exactly what they were! Dikomana—sacred drums.

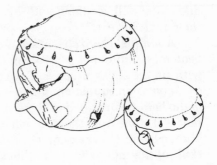

Boshier was well aware that every group of people native to the continent uses drums for some purpose, religious or secular. These range in complexity from ordinary clay pots with wet parchment stretched across their tops, to enormous ceremonial tympani, magnificently carved and elaborately tuned. Some drums are simple objects of percussion, intended for accompaniment to a dance. Others are sophisticated instruments, designed to produce complex tonal sequences for long-distance communication. But both kinds have a way of getting caught up in ceremony and acquiring additional ritual value.

None has gone further along this route than the sacred **koma** drums used in initiation, divination, and rainmaking. These traditionally occur in sets of four or five, which are usually described as a herd, but are known collectively as dikomana, and are played in ceremonies called **komana**.

All koma drums are made from single blocks of soft wood, preferably taken from the trunk of a male marula tree, cut with ceremony and by special permission. The carving is a magical process, generally known as "giving birth to." It is hedged about with strict ritual observances and used to be consecrated by human sacrifice. An old proverb says, "The man who makes the dikomana will see them with his eyes, but he will never hear them with his ears."

A complete herd consists of moradu, "the big cow," which is beaten by hand, and several smaller drums which are played with simple sticks or bones. They are expensive, a herd costing as much as an equivalent number of prize cattle. Each member of the herd is sanctified in some special way, often by inclusion in it of a stone from the stomach of a crocodile or the bone of a human being. Older examples of "the big cow" often contain the skull of the man who made them, and beneath the hide resonator of the smallest drum, it is said, are strips from the same unfortunate artisan's facial skin.

The drums are gods, entrusted to the care of special keepers, whose office is usually hereditary, and who are charged with holding them in a safe place and "feeding" them with oil and fat to keep the drums from cracking or becoming infested with beetles or moths. They are deities that are seldom seen, and beaten only by men initiated into the komana school, on one or two occasions each year, usually at the time of planting. The beating of the sacred drums is said to be "the chief thing that has the power of asking rain from the ancestors."

All this Adrian Boshier knew—and he knew that for these drums to have been left here, rotting and uncared for in a cave, something must have been very, very wrong.

A few weeks later Boshier went down to the village, straight to the home of the modiša. The older man sat, as usual, outside his hut looking out across the southern plains, now almost obscured by the heat haze. Despite the temperature, he was wearing his battered old greatcoat, still fastened with what looked like the same safety pin.

"Sit," he said. And for a while they both sat there and watched as a great number of flies began to gather on the warm mud walls of the hut.

"Do you like flies, modiša?"

"No. They are very bad."

"Then, why don't we kill them while they seem to be sleeping? There must be hundreds here together."

"Oh yes, there are many of them."

"If I took my hat, I could kill at least fifty with one swipe."

"Truly, there are great numbers here."

"Well, shall we do it?"

The older man said nothing for a while. Then he stood up and beckoned Boshier to follow him. They walked a hundred yards up the slope to where the shell of an old settlement brooded among the trees. The modiša told him to go through the broken walls into to what had once been the cattle kraal. This he did, and stood in the center of the empty area for some time, wondering what was supposed to happen and what he should be seeing. When he emerged, the old man asked him what he had seen.

"Nothing in particular."

"Did you see any flies?"

"No. I didn't notice any . . ."

"Of course you didn't, because there aren't any there. The place is dead. It is the place of Mathekga, but he and his people have long since gone. Now there are only spirits. But flies don't follow spirits, they seek warm living people and their animals."

Boshier waited while the keeper of tradition sorted through his mental files.

"Mathekga hated flies. He spent all of his days complaining about them and trying to destroy them. When anyone met Mathekga and greeted him, they knew that his first words would be about the flies that plagued him. Then one day Mathekga came to visit our great chief Matala and, as usual, wasted his breath cursing and swatting flies. Matala grew tired of this behavior and took certain of his elders aside, giving them special instructions.

"The following morning Mathekga heard a sound he knew very well. It was the hoarse and unmistakable bellow of his favorite ox, a great animal that he loved more than any other. He was surprised to hear it there in the village of the chief and even more surprised to see it, together with all his herd, being driven into Matala's kraal. When he confronted his host, the chief simply said, "Go home. You will find your village a much more comfortable place, without flies, now I have taken all your cattle."

The modiša looked hard at Boshier, to see whether he had grasped the moral of the story. "Remember, as you travel through the land, you may judge a man's wealth by the number of his flies. They will warn you when you are approaching a village and what kind of village it is. And they can even, if you are a skillful hunter, tell you when you near your prey."

"Modiša," said Boshier, deliberately and rather rudely changing the subject, "the schools of ordinary initiation are still held for boys and girls, but why are there no koma schools in the Makgabeng? Where are your sacred drums? Do you have no dikomana?"

The older man reeled back as though he had been struck in the face. "How did you know that? Where did you hear it?"

"There are other kinds of schools," Boshier answered. "Other ways of learning. I have read of such drums in books written by people who came here in the old days."

"The missionaries?" asked the old man. And when the visitor nodded, he knew that the worst fears of his fathers had been confirmed. "The *Batoitši*, those from the Berlin Mission Society who came to live with the people of the old chief Malaboch, betrayed our people's trust. They told of our secrets in books. The dingaka were right in wanting to have the white-beards killed. They should have been killed and their bodies fed to the crocodiles."

Boshier was amazed by the violent reaction to his question about the drums, but he persisted. "Are there such drums, modiša? Are there dikomana?"

There was a long silence while the older man scuffled in the sand with the toe of his rubber sandal, the sort millions of Africans fashion from abandoned tires. "There is no hope for our people," he said, "when even our feet defile the land with the tracks of the white man's motorcar."

The modiša seemed to come to a decision. "There were such drums," he said carefully. "A herd that brought great fortune to our people. This place was known then, not as Makgabeng—'the place of Makga'—but Magalabeng—'the place of plenty.' Always the bellies of the people were full. They were fat like the land. But then the missionaries came. They taught us of their god, who was more powerful it seemed than even our greatest spirits. They told us it was wrong to worship any other gods and they made us destroy our shrines, our masks and costumes, and stop using the old ways. And in particular they insisted that we burn the sacred drums."

"Did you?"

"We were afraid of what they and their god and the government would do."

"Did you burn the drums?"

The modiša looked uncomfortable, but said nothing. And the Boshier knew what had to be done.

"Modiša," he said, "can you ask the chief to call a special council? Can you persuade him to summon all the elders from all the villages in the Makgabeng to meet in a kgotla? Can you do this?"

"For what reason?"

"To discuss the rain again. I believe there are things we can do about the drought."

The older man looked at him doubtfully, but he drew hope from something he felt going on behind Boshier's eyes. He stood and walked over to the side of his hut and looked up into the mountains. He saw a solitary black eagle soaring high on a warm draft of air. And above Thaba Godimo hovered a small dark cloud no bigger than a man's hand.

"It can be done," the modiša said.

Mogolwane—

"The elders"

All morning the summons of the meeting drums rolled across the plain of the Makgabeng. In answer the men came from their homes and fields across the dusty landscape in twos and threes, walking in from all directions, each taking his appointed place squatting on the floor of the kgoro. Soon the gathering place was a garden of faces. The men were arranged in groups of *bale-kane*, literally "those who eat together," friends and neighbors who cooperated with each other rather than relatives or clan members. There was much greeting and teasing, but beneath it all a somber tone, a sharing of the hardships produced by the drought.

The common question they were asking was, "What are they eating over there?" The invariable reply was, "They are being killed by hunger." Nobody doubted that the meeting had something to do with the failure of the rains.

When the kgoro was filled to capacity, the drums stopped, and with them, all conversation. A line of elders, the white-haired men from all the villages in order of birth, came filing into the enclosure to sit in rows on either side of the ceremonial hearth on which a small fire burned. Then the blind chief was carried in.

"*Morena!* Great chief!" shouted the men.

"*Ditau,*" he responded. "I am surrounded by lions."

When all was quiet, it was the modiša who got to his feet. He had shed his old coat and was wearing a breastplate of burnished copper suspended from a leather thong around his neck. In his right hand he carried the spirit broom of a ngaka.

"The spirits stand," he said in a loud voice. "And they have been stirred to anger." There was a mutter of agreement.

"We are burned dry by the sun and buffeted by the winds of wrong burials."

"It is so," said the people.

"We have done those things necessary to keep the ancestors happy. We have observed the taboos. We have cleansed the land, held the hunt, and built the rain kraal. But still no frogs cry."

He turned directly to the men in the yard, "We wish to know the reason!"

A man so old that his hair had fallen and all that was left were two white tufts, like horns above his ears, rapped his stick on the ground to attract attention and was helped to his feet by those on either side of him. "I hear the people crying," he said in a soft clear voice. "And I have watched our diviners seek in vain for the cause of the drought. These are good people, skilled in the matters of healing herbs and in hearing the voice of the bones, but they are young. They have not lived as I have, since a time before taxes, when we paid tribute instead in thatching grass and building poles to the great chief Matala. In those days even the Ndebele of Sebetiela came to us for rain. They came because in these mountains of the Makgabeng we were the children of *mašianoke a selwana,* the royal bird, the umber one."

The old man paused and looked around, nodding to emphasize the magnitude of what he had just said. "Mašianoke lives in the ocean. When the seven stars of Selemela rise in the east before the sun, the Lightning Bird takes up water in his mouth to form clouds in the sky and then flies inland in their midst. The wind and rain precede him. Lightning is the flashing of his eyes and thunder the beat of his wings as he passes by."

In the gathering place, nobody moved.

"He comes to our mountains to produce his young. Not in the great nests you have seen on cliffs or trees; these are where he rests during the day. But in the brightness of his urine which falls to the ground and sinks deep down into caves where it is guarded by the great serpent. There the young birds grow. In the summer, when the fireflies dance in the night, the Lightning Bird returns with great flashing to frighten the people so that they cannot see him taking his children away.

"For years now we have watched lightning in the distance but there has been no rain. Mašianoke looks for his young in the mountains of the Gananwa, along the rivers of the Bakwena, in the plains of the Ndebele, but he cannot find them. And until he does, he will not return to the ocean and there will be no rain."

The old man put both hands on the head of his stick and rested for a while. There was movement and whispered conversation among the men. Someone near the back said aloud, "Tell us, then, grandfather, what is it you want us to do?"

The old man let them wait until the moment was right, then looked up and said, "There is a way. When I was young a moroka pula of our people had a whistle made from the wing bone of the Lightning Bird itself. When heavy clouds appeared overhead, he would blow it many times and shout, 'What has angered you? Don't frighten us, just give us water. You who own the water and guard it with thunder, let it rain!'

"There is however no one among us who has such an instrument any longer." There was another of his masterful pauses and he came then, finally, to his punch line. "But, there is another way. There is here someone who is familiar with mašianoke, who also stands alone—someone who is kin to the Lightning Bird."

He flung one arm out in a dramatic gesture without actually pointing, because to do so would have been impolite, and said, "Rradinoga!"

Despite the fact that he had engineered the gathering, Boshier had not expected to be thrown into the limelight so soon. Once there, though, he decided to take advantage of the situation.

"People," he said, "you know me. You've seen my footprints in the mountains and know that I sleep in the caves of your fathers, that I walk in the valleys with the spirits of your ancestors, that I catch and subdue the great snakes of Makgabeng.

"I will tell you why I do these things. I follow the path of moya, the way of the wind, for this is my way. It is the way also of the spirits and they have led me to a thing of great importance—something that explains their anger and their unwillingness to hear your pleas for rain.

"Up in the mountains, not more than a few hours' walk from here, is a cave hidden behind a small door in the rock. And in this cavern is a thing of shame, a blasphemy and a disgrace for all your people, an insult to your ancestors. Standing there, with their bodies being eaten by insects and their dress rotting away with damp, are your gods, dying of neglect."

There was a stirring in the gathering, a growing blend of interest and outrage. He could see that even the modiša, who believed in him, was beginning to understand what was coming, and was aghast. And he knew that he had to make this work, or lose everything.

"There, in that cave, is a treasure greater than all the cows in the chief's kraal—a thing that belongs to every one of you, a thing which was made with honor by your ancestors, who knew its praises and showed it proper respect. It is something that is part of your history and your heritage, which no one here in this kgoro, with the possible exception of these graybeards around me, has ever heard or seen."

Boshier was no longer afraid, no longer treading as carefully as perhaps he should, because he was genuinely angry—so much so that he even forgot the taboo against pointing at the mountains.

"There, in that dusty cave, are your dikomana, an entire herd of five sacred drums." His voice rose to a shout, "Why have you abandoned them?"

A collective gasp—a great wind compounded of anger, distress, astonishment, and incredulity—swept through the gathering. Several older men were on their feet shouting for attention, other younger ones checking with their neighbors, seeking clarification, asking about dikomana. Everyone was disturbed by Boshier's outburst.

The uproar grew, and through the tangled branches of the stockade Boshier could see women standing in the doorways of their huts, wondering what was going on, hustling their youngest children indoors to safety. Half the gathering was standing, pressing forward to where he stood beside the ceremonial fire. Then, just when he was afraid that he was going to be forced to defend himself physically, the very old man with just two tufts of hair stepped between him and the crowd, and stood there with his stick held high.

The clamor died and when all was still, the old one glared around him fiercely. "What is this? What kind of jackals are you? Have you forgotten your manners?"

Those in the front, in direct line of his anger, shuffled sheepishly and sat down. A few voices were raised again in the rear, but these too subsided as he turned to look at them. Then the old man spoke to Boshier.

"You have seen the drums?" Boshier nodded.

"You are certain that they are dikomana?"

"Yes. I recognize them from a description given by one who came here after the battle of Malaboch."

The old man turned to the modiša tlhamane who sat very still with his eyes down. "You, modiša. What have you to say about this? Is it true?"

The keeper of tradition was clearly under considerable strain. He looked haggard, but said nothing. Then the old blind chief raised his hand.

"Sit down, all of you," he commanded. "I will speak." For a minute or more he sat without moving. Then he raised his clouded eyes to a point somewhere over their heads, and began.

"It was many years ago. When we slaughtered an ox for my

father, the chief, and buried him here where I sit now. When the hair of my mother, the *mohumagadi*, had only just begun to grow again and you had all become the new children of my fireplace. We were first approached by the *baruti*, the missionaries.

"Permission was given for them to live and work here among us. And in the beginning it was good. They taught our children, many of whom are now elders of the people, the ways of the world and made of them a bridge which has served us well. They treated sicknesses which our own dingaka were powerless to heal. They taught us the words and praises of their god, and they made us afraid of him.

"When some among us would not take their religion, they threatened us. 'Unless you do what we say,' they said, 'unless you destroy your shrines and burn your carvings and drums, unless you stop worshiping your ancestors, our god will strike you down. He will turn away the clouds in the sky and dry up the breasts of your women.'

"We were afraid. We had seen some of the things these men could do and we were afraid. We held a gathering such as this and it was decided to do as they wanted. I was a young man then, with no hair on my chin, and I listened to the advice of my councillors. We smashed the shrines of the lilies. We tore down the post of skulls at the entrance to the kgoro. We burned the carvings that stood near the kraal. But when it came to the drums, I could not do it. These were the dikomana that had played every year of my life, that had sung us into great rains and made our people fat and the envy of our neighbors. I could not see them destroyed." The old chief sat for a moment with his head down. The memory and the telling of it were exhausting him. Eventually, however, he lifted his blind eyes and, with an effort, continued.

"I took the modiša tlhamane, the father of the one who now keeps our traditions and leads our dancers, and swore him to secrecy. I told him to take the dikomana himself, by night, and put them in a safe place. And I instructed him to take some old drums, *meropa*, ordinary drums used for dancing, and burn them where the missionaries would be able to see the ashes.

"This was done. Then came the white man's war and the

missionaries left us. But the drums remained hidden. We had become concerned by then about the government, about what they would say if we brought out the old drums and the old ceremonies again. So we did nothing. We continued to live in our way, marrying and giving birth and dying according to custom, but we held no more komana ceremonies, no proper schools of koma initiation.

"And now we have this drought. Now I am sorry that we did not keep all the old ways. But there was a problem. I did not know where the drums were hidden. Nobody knew. The old modiša died before he could even tell his son. He was kicked in the head by a bull that was being cut and he took his secret with him.

"Now it seems," and he looked almost angry, "that it is no longer a secret."

An elder who had not yet spoken got to his feet and said, "If this is true, if the old modiša did conceal the drums in a cave, then he would have taken the necessary precautions. This cave would have been hidden from people by the ancestors. No one could see that cave. It would be invisible."

He glared pointedly at Adrian Boshier. Boshier said nothing, but walked over to the stockade fence where his rucksack was hanging and came to place it directly at the feet of the chief. He opened it slowly, deliberately taking time with the fastenings. Then reaching in very carefully with both hands, he lifted out the smallest of the dikomana drums.

There was a scramble as those in the front row of the crowd fell back away from him, and a deathly silence as he put the drum gently down on the ground.

Nobody dared even to breathe.

Then the old bald elder stepped forward very cautiously and reached out with his stick toward the drum. He hesitated several times in uncertainty, but at length touched the drum very lightly on its handle. There was a soft sound of wood on wood, proving that it was solid. The drum was real.

Everyone remembered to breathe again and a great hubbub consumed the gathering. The old man with the stick, looking like the father of a prodigal son, still stood there, unable to move, feasting his eyes on the drum. In the end, however, he was the first to move. He laid his stick down on the ground and fell on both knees in front of the drum.

Silence fell once again on the kgoro. Very gently he extended his cupped hands and lifting the drum like a chalice, set it in the lap of the chief with just one whispered word—*Pampane*—the praise name of the drum.

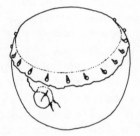

The blind chief ran his hands lovingly over the instrument, feeling the cylindrical handle, touching each of the wooden pegs in turn, caressing the worn head. His milky eyes were turned up to the sky and from the corner of each came a large clear tear that ran down his old cheeks and dropped, audibly, onto the cracked dry membrane of the drum.

When he spoke again it was with decision. "There must be a komana. The herd must be united with its people. All those who have been to circumcision school must be initiated into the koma. They must know the secret and the truth and learn the song of triumph. We will become true men again—men who honor their ancestors. Then there will be rain."

The bent back of the old bald elder straightened with every word of his chief and his voice and bearing were those of a far younger man. "My clan will dress the drums again in new skin covering. A pure black ox without blemish will be slaughtered by a man who is 'healthy' [not sleeping with any of his wives] and we will put the skins on while they are still wet."

Another elder with an unusually long white beard stood up. "While the drums are being renewed, there must be no shouting and no breaking of wood. But my clan will gather together the special sticks used both for beating the drums and the initiates."

The talk seemed to remind each of the elders of some aspect of ritual that was important to the komana and for which he and his family had special responsibility. Each in turn promised the preparation of a lodge that needed to be built, of new pots to hold the beer, of sacred songs to be sung, and even of particular stones that would be hurled at the walls of the huts after dark to frighten the women and keep them indoors.

With the addition of each fragment of the old tradition, the image of the komana grew in the minds of the gathering until the kgoro was filled with a buzz of excitement. Everything seemed to fit into place, to contribute to the picture and the promise it represented, until the modiša stood up to speak in his turn.

"There is something we have forgotten," he said. "What about the blood? We cannot take the drums out again without the blood." And a sudden hard silence descended on the kgoro.

Adrian Boshier had been taking no part in the conversation, simply sitting back and watching the process of spiritual renewal with immense satisfaction. But the mention of blood jerked him back into rapt attention.

Ritual murder had once played an important part in some ceremonies of the Sotho. Boshier knew the stories of the sacrifice of the carver of the dikomana drums, and had heard that human ingredients were still used in the preparation of some rain medicines, but he wanted no part in a revival of this aspect of tradition.

"No!" he objected. "There must be no shedding of human blood. This would cause great trouble."

The modiša hastened to reassure him that there would be no murder. "That ceased among our people long before even the white man arrived. The Mosotho may do these things," he added, in contemptuous reference to the Southern Sotho, "but we do not. The blood we need is something different. Something we used to have but cannot get anymore. There is none of it in this land.

"We need to annoint the drums with it and paint the pots to be used in the komana ceremony. We must renew and dedicate the drums and bring them back to life again, standing with their feet on the ground.

"What we need," he said dramatically, "is the Blood of the Earth."

Phadimo—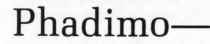

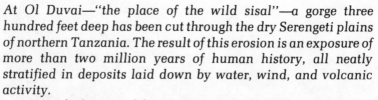

"The glittering stones"

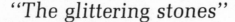

At Ol Duvai—"the place of the wild sisal"—a gorge three hundred feet deep has been cut through the dry Serengeti plains of northern Tanzania. The result of this erosion is an exposure of more than two million years of human history, all neatly stratified in deposits laid down by water, wind, and volcanic activity.

Near the bottom of this geological sandwich is Bed II, which dates from around one and a half million years ago, and contains the remains of three different kinds of early hominid. It has also produced what may be the first evidence of artistic, linguistic, and spiritual evolution.

Lying among some crude stone tools in this bed were found several pieces of red ochre, an oxidized earth containing iron which does not occur naturally in that area. The implication is that these were collected and carried to the site by one or more of the early men. These fragments of iron oxide may have been picked up simply because they were uncommon, because they looked different and caught the eye. But the chances are that there was more to it than that. Three hundred thousand years ago, another early group of hunters took shelter in the Terra Amata cave in what is now southern France. Among their garbage are sixty pencil-shaped pieces of ochre ranging in color from yellow to purple, a variation that can only be produced by heating or firing the natural red ore. Most of the pieces still show signs of abrasion, which suggests that they were made and used as colored crayons, as a source of pigment.

Many animals use simple tools. Some apes in captivity have been persuaded to dabble with paint to produce repetitive patterns. And there are even species of bowerbird that decorate their nest areas with pigments they produce from berries and charcoal. But the preparation and use of ochre as a pigment requires conceptual ability of a different order. It demands recognition and selection of the appropriate minerals, which may have to be excavated or carried for considerable distances. It suggests foresight and creativity in the discovery and use of techniques, such as heating or firing, which induce color changes. It includes the complex procedures involved in abrading or pounding the ore, collecting it in suitable receptacles, and mixing it with water, urine, plant juices, or blood. It also presupposes some powerful motive for going to all this trouble in the first place.

We do not know what the Terra Amata hunters did with their pigment, but judging by later people who lived in similar circumstances, it is likely that they used ochre as a cosmetic. If they did, such patterns on their bodies and faces would have cemented their identity as a group, distinguishing them from all others in the area, helping forge them into a tight interdependent social unit. The application of the colored paste may have been an individual act, or something done for all by a selected member of the group, the first cultural specialist, a forerunner of both the artist and the priest. Its use may have been restricted to just the men or only to those men who hunted, thereby establishing a simple form of ritual.

If the same process was carried over to future hunts it would have become a custom, a cultural pattern, the details of which needed to be memorized or transmitted in some way from person to person—perhaps by speech. It may seem a huge and unjustifiable leap from the mere presence of a piece of colored crayon to a supposition of language, but there are other good reasons for drawing such far-reaching conclusions from the occurrence of red ochre at the sites of early man. We have little concrete knowledge of the hunters of Terra Amata, but when ochre next occurs in the archaeological record, it is quite clear that it has acquired a powerful ritual significance. It is used in burials of the dead.

Deliberate interment, wherever it occurs, implies a concern for the living. And implicit in every funeral practice, no matter how simple, is an awareness that something has changed—a recognition of the fact of death, but also an assumption that it is not the end, that it marks some kind of transition.

Early people must have noticed that the transformation from life very often occurred with loss of blood. And it cannot have escaped their notice that women, the producers of new life, bled in synchrony with the moon, month after month, until such time as the flow of blood was dammed, swelling the belly through the nine critical moons which led to another birth.

It was probably not long after this realization that life and death, blood and birth, came to seem inseparable; this must have led to a belief in the power of blood to regenerate and revitalize. Real blood was undoubtedly the first sacrament and continued through most of human history to be used as a focal point for ceremonies of sacrifice and initiation. It survives still, in symbolic form, in the consecration of wine in sacramental rituals such as the Eucharist. But long before the invention of wine, there was another and more basic symbol, part of earth itself, chosen because of its resemblance to blood.

An Australian aboriginal legend tells how, at the time of creation, the Unthippa women caused blood to flow from their vulvas in such large quantities that it ran into the ground and formed the world's deposits of red ochre. Some coastal people in Australia still mount major expeditions of seventy men and more to cross hundreds of miles of hostile outback to sacred ochre sites laid down in the Dreamland, sites that can be mined only by initiated old men who crawl to them on all fours.

Red ochre today is widely known as bloodstone or hematite (from the Greek haima = blood) and it seems certain that most early people who noticed its resemblance to the hues of fresh or dried human or animal blood drew similar comparisons and conclusions. They therefore used it as a ritual replacement for blood that had been spilled.

One of the earliest known burials in the northern hemisphere is that of an old man, a severely arthritic Mousterian Neanderthal who died forty-six thousand years ago. He was buried in a cave at La Chapelle-aux-Saints in southern France and his body was packed around with red ochre. Similar burials are recorded from nearby La Ferrassie and from Qafzeh and Skhul in Israel. Bodies were either placed on a bed of red ochre or had their dry bones painted with ochre before being buried again at some later date. The thirty-five-thousand-year-old "Red Lady of Paviland" can still be seen at the University Museum in Oxford, encrusted in red ore which "colored the earth for half a yard around."

This connection between ochre and the dead seems to be pandemic. In Africa ochre is still closely connected with custom, ritual, and tradition. It is rubbed into hair, onto bodies, into pottery, carvings, musical instruments, and weapons. It is used medicinally, often smeared on rashes and burns. It is painted over walls, houses, and graves and even sprinkled on the ground, but its use is never casual. It is intimately associated with ceremonies of fertility, initiation, accession, and the request for rain.

The conclusion seems inescapable that throughout his history man has been attracted to colored iron ores, and in particular to red ochre, because it looks like blood. It has become symbolic of blood. We were baptized in the Blood of the Earth.

In 1964 the Swaziland Iron Ore Development Company completed negotiations with Japan which led to the mining and sale of fifty million tons of rich hematite from a mountain on its western border known locally as Emabomvini, "the place of the red." Today the mile-high ridge has been reduced to a massive hole in the ground and the miners have moved on to knock other mountains down. Peace has been restored to the area, but this was not the first time it had been disturbed.

The modern miners were following old tracks. The whole area was so thickly strewn with ancient stone implements that crews on the Japanese bulk carriers amused themselves on the long sea voyage to the East by picking artifacts out of the ore. The ancient tools were of stone foreign to the site, but so plentiful that the miners joked that Japan might receive more dolerite than the hematite they were paying for. When word of these finds reached Johannesburg, Raymond Dart hustled Adrian Boshier off to Swaziland to have a look. Following in the wake of the bulldozers there, Boshier discovered that the stone tools were not confined to the surface layers, but were scattered in their thousands throughout huge depressions in the ground which should have been solid hematite. They were lying among and beneath thousands of tons of red iron oxide, down to a depth of forty feet and more.

Most of these doleritic intrusions were chipped and flaked into rounded and elongated shapes reminiscent of picks, hoes, chisels, and cleavers. It seemed to Boshier that they were specialized tools quite unlike those normally found on a Stone Age living site. He wondered whether those who made and used them had not in fact been after the same prize as the bulldozers. Perhaps they, too, had been mining the rich red iron ore.

The idea of people who had no iron themselves, using stone tools to mine the metal long before the Iron Age, was a difficult one to sell to most archaeologists. But not to Raymond Dart. Thirty-five years earlier, at a site near Broken Hill in what is now Zambia, Dart had investigated some ancient workings and announced the discovery of a Stone Age manganese mine. His discovery had been greeted with widespread skepticism because he dated it at five thousand years, which made it roughly contemporary with known Neolithic activity in Europe, where mining is supposed to have begun with the need for better stone axes to clear forest ground for agriculture. And when Dart made his announcement in 1934, it was generally assumed that mining had been introduced to southern Africa only a thousand years ago, with the spread of Bantu-speaking Iron Age people and their new techniques.

The tools Dart found in Zambia were identical to the ones Boshier brought back from Swaziland. In the former case, the miners seem to have been after pyrolusite, soft and pure crystals of manganese dioxide formed in ancient lake deposits and never used in sub-Saharan Africa, but much valued in Egypt and Mesopotamia. The mineral was used in the north to dye woven fabrics in a whole range of regal colors, from amethyst to purple, to tint glazes, and to render ordinary glass colorless by washing out the usual greenish or brownish hues. It was sufficiently valuable to send expeditions sailing down the east coast of Africa and traveling into the center of the continent five thousand years ago to find it.

It was, in fact, Adrian Boshier who discovered a rock painting that seems to give the first good clue to the true identity of these traders. On the wall of a cave in the Makgabeng he found a mural showing a group of figures apparently dressed in loose full-sleeved garments and wearing what look like turbans on their heads. All five of them are shown bending from the waist in a typical formal Oriental bow. We have no way of knowing whether these foreigners discovered the source for themselves, or were led to it by the local Stone Age people, who decided— or were persuaded—to dig the ore out for the ancient traders.

At first it was assumed that a similar situation must have prevailed in Swaziland, but later Boshier found material that made it possible to identify the aims of the early miners and to date their activities.

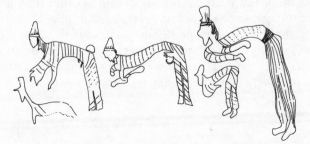

Much of the infilling that the miners poured laboriously back into the holes and adits was solid hematite, which suggested that they were looking for something else as well. They would not have needed to tunnel forty feet into the mountain in order to find an ore lying right on the surface. The answer came when Boshier and a geologist were examining a tunnel with the aid of a carbide lamp. The expert had been invited to see if he could deduce some reason for the old mine. After a while he gave up, saying that all he could see was specularite, a kind of hematite that crystallizes out in the form of glistening, black metallic flakes in a soapy ground. That, of course, is exactly what the miners were after. Further excavation in the floor of that tunnel turned up several stone pestles and mortars, the latter still containing traces of ground pigment.

Once it was pointed out to them, the local Swazi recognized it as a substance they know as ludumane, "the thunder four times." This is something of great power, which only chiefs and the most highly qualified priest-diviners are permitted to wear, smearing their whole bodies and hair with the shining powder. Many other people in Africa know it as sebilo and regard it with similar reverence.

This revelation that the miners were in search of pigments rather than metals was the necessary clue. The discovery made sense of the apparently contradictory situation in which a Stone Age people seemed to be involved in an Iron Age pursuit. It led to a suspicion that this kind of mining might have been going on for longer than anyone suspected.

Charcoal nodules from some of the deeper layers in an ancient Swaziland adit were collected and sent to Yale and Gröningen Radiocarbon Laboratories for dating. The results came in the form of a telegram of congratulation on the discovery of the oldest known mine in the world—an extraordinary forty-five thousand years in age—seven times older than what was then thought to be the oldest evidence of mining activity, a hole dug for flint in Europe. Since then, evidence has been collected from this and other sites, suggesting that the origins of mining in Africa may go back even further, perhaps as far as one hundred and forty thousand years, for there seems to have been a sudden widespread demand at about that time for colored and glittering minerals.

These discoveries have made it necessary to revise the entire Stone Age chronology for sub-Saharan Africa, pushing it back two or three times as far as it was once believed to go. Africa now appears to be not so much the cultural cul-de-sac it was long supposed to be, but the center of technological invention and innovation during much of the one hundred thousand years that preceded the agricultural revolution in Europe.

The finds have also synthesized our understanding of the origins of ceremony and symbology. For in the Swaziland mine the excavators found the skeleton of a child buried at least fifty thousand years ago, together with a perforated seashell pendant. This is the first recorded evidence of personal adornment, which suggests aesthetic appreciation and, with the shape of the skull, confirms beyond doubt that the miners were true men— modern Homo sapiens and not the Boskop-Neanderthal types who were, it was once supposed, the only inhabitants of Africa at the time.

The finds not only have doubled the antiquity of modern man but they have shown that his genesis and formative history must now be regarded as confined to Africa. It was here that his more complex brain came into being, making possible a new capacity for self-awareness, which led him to question the purpose of individual existence and the nature of human destiny.

Raymond Dart, as usual, saw things in their broadest perspective. "Hematite has a fantastic cultural evolutionary history, beginning with Mousterian burial ritual and extending through its manifold late Paleolithic artistic, religious, trading, and bartering applications. By means of its dominating agency in the diffusion of the myths, rites, and mysteries of ancient metallurgy and alchemy, it has played parts of such continuity and expanding diversity as to have rendered it unique among all minerals in molding mankind's existence then and today."

The customs and beliefs about red ochre, and about specularite in particular, have become so fixed and so widespread that they still dominate the religious thought of even literate peoples. It is clear that increasing familiarity with the substances over the millennia is what provoked purposeful mining and began a process that has conditioned all of prehistory and determined much of the direction taken by our industrial society. Red ochre in effect sparked off the first, and in many ways the most fundamental, of our iron revolutions. The Industrial Revolution of the eighteenth and nineteenth centuries was an eventual consequence of this early breakthrough, but in comparison to the birth of true self and social consciousness it was nothing more than a technical innovation.

We are deeply embedded in the earth, particularly the red earth of Africa, which not only cradled life at its inception, but continues to act as a cultural catalyst.

Having been intimately involved in the Swaziland discoveries, Adrian Boshier was better prepared than almost anyone alive to deal with the need of the people of the Makgabeng for the "Blood of the Earth." Not only did he know what it was, but where to find it as well. He went to fetch some.

Lebone—

*"The lamps of
the seers"*

Earth bleeds when red-hot intrusions of igneous rock force themselves up into the crust accompanied by superheated water that throws the thin skin into blisters. Hydrothermal solutions within these raised areas settle out into concentric layers with the ores, like iron, which melt at the lowest temperatures, furthest away from the core. Those actually at the surface are rapidly oxidized, producing the typical bright red colors of most iron deposits. Hematite often crystallizes out in a steel-gray tabular form with a brilliant luster that has come to be known as specularite, iron glance, or looking-glass ore. But closer to the surface it becomes more earthy, more brightly colored, and is known as soft red ore, ruddle, or red ochre.

Ochre occurs in a number of grades and shades, but the one most favored as a pigment by people in Africa is a soft, almost soapy form that needs little extra grinding and produces the most vivid blood colors. This is the true Blood of the Earth.

Adrian Boshier collected two tons of it from the ancient

mine at Emabomvini in Swaziland, taking great care to observe all the necessary rituals: digging it out only from the top of the mountain, furthest away from *inkanyamba*, the temperamental, horned great serpent god of the underworld; making the customary offerings of water, meal, and tobacco left behind in clay pots at the workings; and filling in the resulting hole with rubble, because the skirts of the ravaged earth must be decently rearranged.

He loaded the precious cargo onto a truck and drove it more than three hundred miles across the highveld to the Makgabeng, reviving once again an ancient trade. He was opening up a route that had been traveled for hundreds, perhaps even thousands of years by a people that Bantu describe as "tall and other colored." He was bringing back a commodity that had been missing from an economy for several generations. In the process he was reviving a culture.

As soon as Boshier arrived at the village, the people gathered around to examine his gift. The ochre was passed from hand to hand by the old ones, both men and women, who rubbed it critically between their fingers, feeling the texture, assessing its rusty smell, and even tasting a little with the tip of the tongue. There was a considered exchange of looks and a carefully measured consensus of nods among them before the modiša delivered his verdict.

"It is good. This is the true *letsoku*. This is indeed the very blood of our mother earth." And so the whole process of celebration and renewal began.

First the ochre was finely ground by four old women, all of them, Boshier later discovered, powerful dingaka. They worked together on old grindstones which had been excavated from some secret hiding place and washed especially for this purpose. As they ground, all kneeling in a line in the courtyard of the old blind chief, they sang:

> *Unlocker of gates that are blocked,*
> *Defender of the mountain;*
> *New sky of a dawning day,*
> *Great red ox of the morning;*
> *Roaring like thunder, this marvelous beast,*
> *Tears up the fringe-skirts of the rain.*

Then the bright red powder was distributed among those who would need to use it. Word was passed among all the people that no sticks must be broken, on pain of the fine of an ox, and no one must shout or beat a drum.

Early the following morning a procession formed up at the entrance to the kgoro. The men were in front, leading a pure black bull; behind them came all the women dressed in long goatskin skirts reaching down to their ankles and decorated in beads. One old woman carried a whitewashed calabash of beer.

Everyone walked together down to the dry riverbed and across it to a single hut in an unusually thick patch of bush. In the doorway stood Rrasebe. On her head she wore a crown of goatskin, and stuck into the beaded bands on her upper arms were two enormous ostrich plumes. She wore white gloves and in her right hand carried a calabash rattle mounted on a stick, like a mace. In her left hand was the spirit broom of a high ngaka.

Under her direction the bull was taken to a nearby thorn tree and its neck tied close to the trunk. All the men gathered close to it clapping rhythmically and the women, standing well in the background, took up their shimmering cry of praise. This is the liquid, trembling, high-pitched sound that anthropologists identify with the flat, clinical name of ululation. It is much more than that. It is a fervent cry that can put fire into the blood even of a dead man and is normally reserved for the return of a conquering hero, but this time it was given in honor of the bull.

As the sound soared across the clearing, one of the elders felled the animal with a single blow from a huge hammer stone, struck right between the horns. Then the animal's throat was slit and its blood collected in a large wooden bowl. When the right amount had flowed, Rrasebe joined the group gathered round the sacrificial animal and placed a pot of water by its side. She clapped once, knelt at the bull's head, and carefully, even tenderly, washed its forehead and face. Then she rose and clapped her hands, just once again.

A group of women came forward carrying leafy branches of mokhokhothoane—a tree with grapelike edible fruit—and laid these down in a small square carpet on the sand. The bull's head was severed completely and placed with some reverence on this green shrine. Beer was poured over it while the men skinned the rest of the animal, carefully preserving the hide for use on the komana drums.

Next they opened the abdomen and, with their bare hands, separated and brought out several pounds of the pure fat that hangs from a membrane below the stomach and colon. This was placed in the bowl of blood for mixture later with the ochre that would be used to paint the drums. A huge fire was built nearby and, apart from several pieces of meat cut from the inner side of each forelimb for placing on the graves of former chiefs, along with the entrails, the entire carcass was lightly roasted and eaten by all the people, with no salt, but with great and obvious pleasure. As evening drew on, the procession returned the way it had come, though this time with laughter and song.

On the second day Adrian Boshier took a small group of the elders, all of whom had already been through the koma school as young men, up to the cave of the drums. None of the old men could climb up into the narrow defile, so Boshier carried the drums down one by one to the sandy floor of the valley below. And there the white-haired elders fell on their knees before the sacred herd and wept, both for the joy of reunion and for the sadness of the many years that had passed since they had seen the drums.

Each of the men carried one of the drums on the journey back down the mountain and when they came within sight and sound of the village, one of them blew several long blasts on an antelope horn trumpet. The women and children all disappeared indoors and a phalanx of older men came out to act as a screen for the drums. They marched in front and at the sides of the group, whistling and throwing stones to warn the people that they must not be out.

The drums were carried to a grass hut that had been specially built to house them in a clearing on the far side of the village. Here they were placed on a smooth dung floor, heavily sprinkled with powdered ochre. And here the men of the clan responsible for dressing them again, set to work, cleaning and repairing, polishing the wood with fat and ochre, replacing the worn skins with new hide from the sacrificial black bull and pegging it down with new wooden "fingers" while the leather was still wet.

In the meantime, the village potters had been busy collecting new white clay and molding it by hand into ropes that were built up in spirals to produce a variety of bowls and pots, all burnished smooth with river pebbles. As these dried in the hot sun, each was polished again and again with the ochre until it glowed, as though lit from within by an orange flame: *lebone,* the lamps of the seers.

The village smith, who turned out to be the modiša himself, practiced his arcane art behind an old stone wall in a valley nearby. Pumping a traditional clay furnace up to the necessary heat with simple leather bellows that blew a stream of air into the charcoal fire, he smelted ground iron ore with a heavy flavoring of powdered ochre. He hammered and shaped the metal into knives that would be used in the initiation.

Preparation continued for an entire week, until the night of the new moon. Then the bustle ceased. Evening meals were eaten early and everyone was ready, waiting in their courtyards or sitting quietly in the kgoro, when the sun went down. As the last rim of the flaming disc disappeared behind the hills beyond the Magalakwena River in the west, as the first bats appeared in the cooling air, the drums began. For the first time in over half a century, the dikomana spoke again. *Moradu,* "the big cow," led the way, throbbing in the growing darkness like the pulse of the earth itself, closely followed by the rest of the herd. The other drums were beaten with sticks in a rolling sequence that built an elaborate rhythmic superstructure on which *pampane,* the smallest one, made brisk and sporadic comment.

The effect was hypnotic. The sound rolled out through the village, rising and falling in waves that washed the soul of every person there. It was impossible not to be moved by the cadence, not to feel that one had heard that song before, or even danced to it around a ceremonial fire.

Adrian Boshier, sitting out in the courtyard of the chief, surrendered himself to the sound and was surprised when he opened his eyes to find himself surrounded by people. In front of the throng was the bald elder. "Who is Lesibe?" the elder asked.

Taken off guard, Boshier thought about it for a while and replied that it was the name of a musical instrument, a peculiarly African stringed-wind instrument consisting of a feather fixed to a bowstring, which is made to resonate in an eerie fashion by blowing over the quill.

"Who is Lesibe?" asked the old man again.

Boshier thought again and ventured that it might perhaps be a feather.

"No," said the elder. "*Lesiba* is a feather. Who is Lesibe?"

He thought and thought again, and remembered that one of the clans of the Makgabeng was known as Masibe. "It's a name," he said.

"Whose name?" the old man persisted.

"I don't know." Everyone laughed.

"Who is Lesibe la Magaganeng?" asked the old man.

"I don't think I know him," replied Boshier. This made everyone laugh very loudly indeed.

Then one of the women in the crowd took pity on him and said, "It's you!"

"It's me?"

"It's you. That's your name!"

"But my name is Rradinoga."

"Yes, your name is Rradinoga, but now your name is also Lesibe." There was no question about whether he wanted to be Lesibe or not. It just was so.

"When did I get that name?"

"For a long time now," the bald one explained, "we have been arguing among ourselves which it should be. I wanted you in my school and they wanted you in theirs, and we had a hard time deciding."

He still did not understand. "You have been arguing about my going to school?"

"Yes, and the Masibe won because there are more of us. The rest of them didn't stand a chance."

"Is it an old school?"

"Ah, a very old school. But only for the wise old ones like you. This one," and here he pointed at a white-haired man old enough to be Boshier's father, "is too young to join."

"And what is la Magaganeng?"

"It means of the caves. Lesibe of the Caves. Everyone who has been accepted by our clan is Lesibe of something. We have never before had a Lesibe of the Caves. Now that is you."

Boshier wanted to know more about what was going on, but he knew better than to ask any further questions. With the people there is a simple rule: Either you are told, or you know already, or it is none of your business. So he just kept quiet.

"The one who told you about the drums," continued the old Masibe, "must have been one of our ancestors. We will have to get his consent." And with that cryptic comment they led him across the river again, with the drums still rolling out behind them, to the house of Rrasebe.

The old woman sat on the floor in the center of the hut, rocking gently back and forth.

"She is with spirit," they explained. Someone added that her spirit was called Peti, but that there was also another called Didi who was off at the moment collecting wild tea up in the mountains.

"Will it be long?" he asked.

"It takes the time it wants." Obviously a silly question. "We wait for it to return, then she is complete again—Rrasebe Mmapeti Mmadidi—mother of all."

For a long while the statuesque woman sat there rocking very slowly while everyone waited. Then suddenly Rrasebe began to sing. She began to make deep, guttural sounds. Several women in the group produced small, tambourinelike *morapana* drums and began to beat them to a monotonous, repetitive rhythm which soon took over everyone in the hut. They even breathed in unison.

Rrasebe began to dance. Though she was an old woman, a great-grandmother, she shed her years like water. She spun and turned, she swayed and pivoted, stamping on the ground, coaxing the drummers on to heights of virtuosity.

Twice she stopped altogether, gesturing imperiously at one of the players whose instrument was flat or off key, waiting until it had been tuned once more with a little heat or water, before she picked up the rhythm again. The spirits, it seemed, insisted on perfection.

For hours she kept dancing. Several times one of the younger women joined in with her for a while, but all of them fell away exhausted as Rrasebe danced relentlessly on.

When she eventually stopped, the incredible old woman,

mother of the mountains, came over to where Adrian Boshier sat entranced, and said, "The spirits welcome you." That was all.

Boshier went back to the village, guided through the dark by the beat of the dikomana drums, which did not stop until long after the pale sliver of moon had gone and the first light of dawn could just be seen, creeping over the mountain wall behind them.

The next day the koma school began and, as a Lesibe, he was automatically enrolled—and beaten. All the initiates gathered after breakfast in the kgoro and were made to run the gauntlet between two rows of elders led by the one with the long white beard, who beat them on their bare backs with special komana sticks. In this way they paid for their tuition. Then they were led into the grass lodge and allowed, most of them for the first time, to see the sacred drums.

For six days they sat there at the feet of the elders, learning the special rites, the koma songs, and the secret whistling language. And in the afternoon of the final day, when all was done, the teachers together made a prolonged sound, "rrrrrrrrrrrrrr," as a sign of the finish and said, "Ho ofa, it is flown. The komana is done."

That night the sacred drums started again and were played, some of them by the new initiates, right through until the dawn. On the seventh day, it rained. Clouds began building over the mountains soon after noon and by early evening there was a dark wall backed up over the Citadel like a wave in suspension, leaving the village in sultry stillness at its feet.

As the sun touched the distant western hills, a convoy of winds blasted across the plain, whipping up clouds of red dust that hung like a pall in the air. Then the lightning flashed, bright and close, and behind the thunder everyone could hear the rain.

A solid wall of water moved slowly along the base of the cliffs, rainbowed against the dark clouds behind it. It hissed and spattered on the parched ground, huge drops at first that set dry leaves dancing, and then a steady downpour that seemed to turn the world itself to mud.

The people rushed out into the fields and courtyards, holding their arms up to the sky, letting the rain run down their faces, rejoicing in the feel and the sound and the smell of the falling water. Most of them stopped in their manic dance to turn for one long, deep, thankful look at the hut in the clearing that had housed the sacred drums.

They were gone now, hidden away once again. But they had done their work.

Part Five

"Water is a thing from which even the earth
cannot keep its secrets."

Sotho proverb.

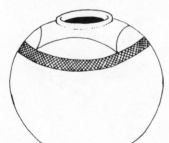

WATER

The use of terms such as "supernatural," with reference to Africa, is misleading. They imply a dichotomy between the "natural" universe, which is subject to the laws of science; and another superimposed realm of the spirit, in which these laws do not operate. This dichotomy is an artifact of our European literate culture; it does not apply to African belief.

A member of a tribal society sees the world as made up of things plain and things hidden, and draws no distinction between them. He understands that they present themselves together, mixed into one common reality. For instance, in the rust-red soil of a bushveld trail, there lies the imprint of a single cloven hoof. A tracker squats easily down beside it on his haunches, examines the depth and shape of the spoor, feels the texture of the soil, and notes the direction and extent to which the surface has been disturbed by the passage of the animal. He concludes that it was made by a kudu antelope, a young female, injured in her left front leg by an unsuccessful attack by a crocodile two hours ago as she drank at a nearby pool. This *we call science.*

The tracker stands over the hoofprint and points at it, palm down with his fingers folded back and thumb spread out at right angles, to hold the spoor in place and keep the antelope from fleeing too far. Then he reaches out to strip a single long white thorn from an acacia growing alongside the trail and plunges this down into the imprint to aggravate the animal's wound. This *we call magic.*

But in Africa it is difficult or impossible to tell the difference. Both proceed on the belief that cause produces effect. A herd of sacred drums, properly annointed with the blood of the earth, is beaten—and it rains. Our training leads us to doubt any such causal connection. You "know" that you cannot make it rain simply by beating on a drum, that wanting something does not necessarily make it happen. Or does it?

Modern physics sees the cosmos as a multiple state system, a closed book with an infinite number of pages. Particular reality, it suggests, does not exist until a reader comes along and opens the book, usually at a well-thumbed page. In the words of quantum mechanics, an observer collapses the system into one of its component states. He is not part of that system and cannot be included in the usual equations used to describe it. But neither can he be left out, because without him there would be no particular pattern, no reality.

It is no longer possible to deny that our thoughts and desires might influence our environment. The most recent cosmologies all include consciousness as an active participating factor in reality. The new explanations of how the world works are strangely like the old beliefs of nonliterate people everywhere. Undogmatic minds are much concerned with magic, and arrive, as a result, at descriptions of reality which to us seem faulty, but may in the final analysis prove to be more meaningful than those we contrive by the elaborate exercise of logic and contingent mathematics. It seems that merely by admitting the possibility of unlikely events, you increase the probability of their occurrence.

In Africa, all diviners who work with the spirits receive some form of baptism by water, or initiation at the hands of water beings—most often the Great Serpent himself who lives at the bottom of a deep river pool. Each person called to be a diviner falls sick and has a dream or trance experience of being taken down into a pool by a snake or by the force of a whirlwind.

The details of the story differ, but in the depths of the pool the initiate meets water spirits, old men or women who seem to represent the ancestors and who are eager to impart the knowledge a diviner will need. They point out something white, most often a stone or a piece of white clay, which will later play a prominent part in the ceremony of coming out. This object is defended by the snake, who may wear it in his forehead like a jewel. According to most versions of the story, this gem must be stolen by some subterfuge, such as blowing snuff in the serpent's eyes.

The initiate always disappears from his or her home and is sometimes found wandering naked, as though newborn, near the water's edge. Often relatives will drive their cattle into a river or pool in the belief that by doing so they stir up the water sufficiently to blind the serpent and force him into releasing the novice. The waters of initiation are never still. They are living waters in a pool at the base of a waterfall or in a river flowing by. "The river is a moving road," say the people. And even those who live far inland know that eventually it leads to the sea, emptying into a space that can never be filled. This is the realm of the dead—the "waters under the sea" that swallow up the living and possess a power against which nothing can be done.

Senyama—

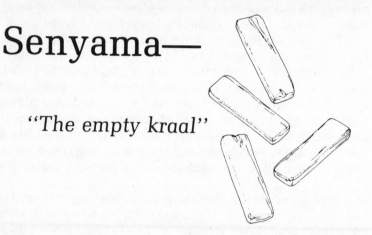

"The empty kraal"

Throughout Africa, on the desert or the forest margins, at major crossroads, or along the crest of hills with long horizons, stand huge cairns of stone.

These are not ancient ruins, but dynamic, living structures that grow and change with time. They are altered by contact with every passerby, who contributes yet another fragment to the never-completed whole.

Some see these cairns as barriers erected by travelers against devils who follow closely in their tracks. The snake crawls around them and is delayed; the lion smells them and fears a trap; and the enemy sees them and stops short, for fear of sorcery.

Others regard them as graves, or as markers erected at a spot where a body has been rested on its way to burial at a distant home.

The real reason for their existence, however, may have something in common with the powerful urge that causes people everywhere to throw coins into fountains, scribble their names on walls, or simply turn to look at their footprints on a beach of fresh, wet sand. It is a need to affirm one's own existence, a way of saying "I too was here."

In Africa they say it with stones. When the sun is hot, or the way is long, or the path unfamiliar, Africans pause for a moment on the edge of the unknown, add a stone to one such growing pile, and say, very simply, "Great Mother, I am passing." Adrian Boshier did just that. In twenty-two years of walking African trails, he left his trace on a number of cairns and concerns. He tossed his stones at random, but many of them hit the mark.

Boshier was instrumental in demonstrating the continued use of simple bone tools for sacred purposes, thus providing evidence supporting the possible prehistoric existence of a Bone Age culture. By his way of life, he showed that even now it is possible for a man alone, unarmed and far from others of his kind, to make a living as a scavenger, stealing food from the mouths of predators.

Although he first became involved with snakes out of simple curiosity, Boshier's later acceptance by tribal people owed a great deal to the reptiles; and drew attention to the continuing significance and survival value of totems in African culture.

Boshier uncovered an unsuspected early trade in special stone for the purposes of pounding, and helped revive an interest in the importance of the process of pounding as a precursor in the development of more sophisticated stone tools. He was aware of the spiritual significance of stone and helped foster an interest in rock gongs as a possible clue to the origins of human dance and song.

He explored the symbolism in prehistoric art, recording a number of important sites, showing that many of these retain their meaning to those who still live in the land. He was involved in work which suggests that one of the earliest known scripts was used in, and may even have evolved in, Africa.

Boshier showed how magic—or, if you will, a belief in magic—can be an essential tool for survival; and he contributed to research that continues to lead toward an understanding of the origins of religion. He discovered the oldest known mine in the world which may well have doubled the antiquity of modern man, showing that our genesis and formative history were peculiarly African. He helped excavate evidence of the first recorded use of personal adornment, demonstrating the early origin of an interest in ceremony and symbology, and making it necessary to revise the entire Stone Age chronology for Africa.

Boshier has, then, been instrumental in leading us to the realization that the African continent was the world center of technological innovation over a hundred thousand years ago. He demonstrated once again the vital importance of pigments, such as red ochre, as cultural catalysts. And he was almost single-handedly responsible for reviving a dying culture.

It must be admitted that Boshier's grasp of many of these areas to which he contributed was not always profound. And he had personal limitations that kept him from any systematic consolidation of his accomplishments. He finished, for example, almost nothing that he started. Yet the things he did accomplish, when seen together and in retrospect, are essential parts of a very broad mosaic, which teaches us much about Africa. And, because of that continent's vital role in human history, Boshier's findings tell us a great deal about ourselves.

Furthermore, Adrian Boshier's accomplishments are all the more remarkable when we consider the brevity of his life; the fact that his formal education ended in secondary school; and that he had constantly to fight the personal and cultural imped-iments raised by being epileptic.

In every field in which he was involved—paleontology, prehistoric art, cultural anthropology, herpetology, mining history, and witchcraft—there exist many experts who possess greater and more comprehensive knowledge than Adrian Boshier. Yet he was able in a strange way to bring something new to all their studies. His contribution was something undisciplined and personal, and quite distinct from the colonial attitudes of much modern research that still carries an implicit assumption of "us" and "them."

Adrian Boshier was definitely one of "them."

　　By early 1978, Adrian Boshier was having as many as thirty epileptic attacks a week. His health and strength deteriorated rapidly and, with them, his morale. He became quieter, more gentle, less extroverted, and subject to long bouts of acute melancholy.

　　Rrasebe and other dingaka pleaded with him to resume his training, but there was something about this necessarily inward journey that made it too risky for him to undertake. He tried desperately to put his story down on paper, but the energy that had gone into the living was somehow lost in the telling; and this made him more depressed than ever.

　　On November 18, 1978, he went, against his will, on a trip with friends to the shores of the Indian Ocean. In warm, clear water on the very edge of the narrow continental shelf, the Lightning Bird arched its back, beat its wings, and returned to its birthplace in the deep. Adrian Boshier struggled for a moment at the surface, then sank slowly, almost gratefully, into the void.

He did not drown; but when they brought him back to the surface, he was dead.

The next day, they say, an enormous dark bank of cloud came sailing up out of the far southeast to run itself aground on the slopes of Those-Who-Point-Will-Never-Reach-Their-Homes. Then lightning flashed, the thunder roared, and it rained and rained and rained in the dry Makgabeng.

Glossary

Most of the events described here took place in the northern Transvaal, in areas inhabited by people belonging to the cultural group known as Northern Sotho. This is a gathering of traditional chiefdoms that share a common lineage, but whose people speak a variety of Bantu dialects. All, however, now share a common written language based on old *Sepêdi*. The orthography and forms used here are of this new *Sesotho*, as decided on by the Sotho Language Board.

It will be noticed that, with very few exceptions, all syllables in Northern Sotho end in a vowel, and where this is raised or accented, it is marked with a circumflex, "só." The h in Northern Sotho is heavily aspirated. The g is guttural, like the Scottish "ch" in loch. And where the s is pronounced like the English "sh," it is marked with a breve and written š.

The term *Bantu*, which literally means "the People," has unfortunately acquired political overtones and fallen into disfavor among the people themselves. The preferred form of "African" does not, however, distinguish between those who now occupy the majority of the continent and others, such as the KhoiSan (a collective name for the Khoi or "Hottentots" and the San or "Bushmen") who preceded them.

So until this awkward gap in terminology is filled, it is still necessary to use "Bantu"—on the clear understanding that it has here no pejorative meaning and is simply the most convenient way of describing a number of black African people who share a group of related languages.

All Northern Sotho words used in the text, including some proper nouns, are listed below with their meanings and derivations:

babelegisi Midwives (plural of *mmelegisi*)
badimo Spirits of the ancestors (plural of *modimo*)
bahlabani Soldiers, armed men (plural of *mohlabani*)
balekane Mates, fellows (plural of *molekane*)
bana Children (plural of *ngwana*)
baruti Missionaries (plural of *moruti*)
Batoitši Germans
bina To dance or worship by dancing
bogobe Maize porridge, staple food
bohlale Wisdom, cunning
bolata State of being a layman
bollo Hot
bophelo Life, soul
bosenaselo Nothingness
dibe Sins (plural of *sebe*)
dikomana Drums used at a secret ceremony
dinaledi Stars (plural of *naledi*)
dinaleng Communal grindstone
dingaka Diviners (plural of *ngaka*)
ditaola Knucklebones, art of divination (plural of *taola*)
ditau Lions (plural of *tau*)
dumela Agree, believe, acknowledge
go With, to
godimo High, above
kgabo Monkey, baboon (*Papio ursinus*)
kgadi Appear for an instant
kgolo Great, important
kgoro Courtyard, meeting place for men
kgosi Chief
kgotla Meeting place for chief and his councillors
kgwedi Moon, month
kiba To beat time with the foot, to dance
kolobe Pig
kololo Klipspringer antelope (*Oreotragus oreotragus*)
koma Secret, song of triumph, initiation school

komana Secret ceremony
kwena Crocodile (*Crocodylus niloticus*)
lahla Discard, throw away
lebenkele Shop
lebone Lamp, torch
Leburu Boer
ledibogo Ford, drift
leeto Journey, voyage
lefoka Plot of grass, undergrowth
lehu Death, plague
Leisimane Englishman
lekgolo One hundred, a century
lengana Wild wormwood (*Artemisia afra*)
lengwe One other
lesiba Feather
letsatsi Sun, heat, drought
letsoku Red ochre, hematite
lotša Greet, salute
lwala Millstone
mafiroane Baboon-tail plant (*Vellozia equisetoides*)
magosi Chiefs (plural of *kgosi*)
Makolobe The stars of Orion's belt (plural of *kolobe*)
mašianoke Hamerkop bird (*Scopus umbretta*)
maswi Milk, buttermilk
meropa Drums (plural of *moropa*)
mme Mother
mmelegisi Midwife
mmilo Wild medlar (*Vangueria infausta*)
Modimo God, spirit
modiša Shepherd, pastor, guardian
mofediši One who puts an end to things, African ebony (*Diospyros mespiliformis*)
mogolwane Elder brother, elder sister
mohlabani Soldier
mohlare Tree
mohlasana Diminutive tree
Mohlodi The Creator, the eye of a fountain
mohloko Milkwort plant (*Polygala gymnocladia*)
mohumagadi Queen
mokasani Sweat bees of genus *Nomia*
mokgogopha Succulent plant of genus *Euphorbia*
mokgopha Succulent plant of genus *Aloe*
mokhokhotoane Live-long tree (*Lannea discolor*)

molekane Equal, mate
moloi Sorcerer
moradu An old animal, a big cow
morara Vine (*Clematis brachiata*)
morena Lord, chief, master
morokapula Rainmaker
moropa Drum
morula Marula tree (*Sclerocarya caffra*)
moruti Missionary
morutiwa Student, disciple, apprentice
moya Air, breath, wind, spirit
muwe Bird plum tree (*Berchemia discolor*)
Naka The star Canopus, a horn
naledi Star
ngaka Diviner, healer, herbalist
ngwana Child, infant
nkwe Leopard (*Panthera pardus*)
noga Snake
noka River
noko Porcupine (*Hystrix cristata*)
patolo Sharpening stone (or *kgekgeto*)
peetla Cobra of genus *Naja*
pela Rock hyrax, dassie (*Procavia capensis*)
phadimo Glittering, luster
phaga Common genet (*Genetta genetta*)
phokolo Weakness, hardship
phuti Duiker antelope of genus *Sylvicapra*
pula Rain
ralebenkele Shopkeeper
rra (ra) Father
Rra-bophelo Father of Life
Rra-dinoga Father of Snakes
Rra-lehu Father of Death
Rrasebe Father of Sin
sebe Sin
sebete Liver, courage
segoko Spider
Selemela Constellation of the Pleiades
selwana Small thing
senthulo Hornless cattle, pollard
senyama Misfortune, bad luck
serapa Garden
sereto Song of praise, praise-name, tribal name

siboko   totem (or *seano*)
taola   Knucklebone
tau   Lion
temoso   Warning
thaba   Mountain, rejoice
thakadu   Aardvark (*Orycteropus afer*)
tlhamane   Tradition
Toitši   German
tšilo   Grindstone
umsenge   Cabbage tree (*Cussonia paniculata*)
Waburu   Boers (plural of *Leburu*)

Boshier
Bibliography

1. Beaumont, P. B., and Boshier, Adrian. "Some Comments on Recent Findings at Border Cave, Northern Natal," *South African Journal of Science*, *68*: 22–24, 1972.
2. Beaumont, P. B., and Boshier, Adrian. "Report on Test Excavation in a Prehistoric Pigment Mine Near Postmasburg, Northern Cape," *South African Archaeological Bulletin*, *29*: 41–59, 1974.
3. Boshier, Adrian. "Mystery of Rock Painting," *The Star*, Johannesburg, June 8, 1962.
4. Boshier, Adrian. "First Transvaal Rock Painting of Domestic Animals," *The Star*, Johannesburg, Sept. 6, 1962.
5. Boshier, Adrian. "Ancient Mining of Bomvu Ridge," *Scientific South Africa*, *2*: 317–320, 1965.
6. Boshier, Adrian. "Effects of Pounding by Africans of North-West Transvaal on Hard and Soft Stones," *South African Archaeological Bulletin*, *20*: 131–138, 1965.
7. Boshier, Adrian. "Madame Witchdoctor," *Perspective*, *3*: 15–17, 1966.
8. Boshier, Adrian. "Mining Genesis," *Mining Survey*, *64*: 21–28, 1969.

9. Boshier, Adrian. "A Note on the Masetedi," *South African Journal of Science,* 68: 206–208, 1972.
10. Boshier, Adrian. "Swaziland: a Birthplace of Modern Man," *Science Digest:* 42–47, March 1973.
11. Boshier, Adrian. "African Apprenticeship," *Parapsychology Review,* 5: 1–27, 1974.
12. Boshier, Adrian. "ESP amongst African Priest-diviners," *Odyssey,* 1, 1977.
13. Boshier, Adrian. "The Earliest Miners," *South African Journal of Africana,* 1: 9–10, 1978.
14. Boshier, Adrian. "The Religions of Africa." In *Life After Death,* Hodder & Stoughton (London, 1976).
15. Boshier, Adrian, and Beaumont, P. B. "Mining in Southern Africa and the Emergence of Modern Man," *Optima,* Johannesburg, 1972.
16. Boshier, Adrian, and Beaumont, P. B. "Beyond the Mists of Mining," *Nuclear Antiquity,* 2: 21–26, 1974.
17. Boshier, Adrian, and Costello, Darby. "Witchdoctor," Museum of Man and Science, Johannesburg, 1975.
18. Boshier, Adrian, and Costello, Darby. "Witchdoctor," *The Flying Springbok,* October 1977.

Index

Outstanding Paperback Books from the Touchstone Library:

☐ **Life Itself**
By Francis Crick
The Nobel Prize-winning biologist takes us on a fascinating journey of discovery into the ultimate scientific question: what is the nature and origin of life itself?
25563-0 $4.95

☐ **The Universe Within**
By Morton Hunt
This stunning work invites us to explore the dazzling mystery of the human mind in "the most complete, factual, and imaginative presentation of the field…"
—Los Angeles Times.
25259-3 $9.95

☐ **Other Worlds**
By Paul Davies
In this "luminously clear and tremendously exciting" book (Isaac Asimov), Davies explores the astonishing implications of the quantum theory of the universe, drawing conclusions that challenge our assumptions about the nature of time and space.
42232-4 $5.15

☐ **Human Navigation and the Sixth Sense**
By R. Robin Baker
In a clear and elegant style, the noted zoologist offers compelling evidence for a sixth sense in humans that parallels the innate sense of direction long known to exist in many animals.
44129-9 $4.95

☐ **The Edge of Infinity**
By Paul Davies
Described by Publishers Weekly as "intensely imaginative," *The Edge of Infinity* reveals an entire new era of physics, exploring the origin, and ultimate end, of the universe.
46062-5 $6.95

☐ **The Foundations of Ethology**
By Konrad Lorenz
This unique overview of the fascinating field of ethology, by its most creative pioneer, addresses the truly controversial questions concerning the similarities and differences between animal, and human behavior.
44573-1 $9.95

- - - - - - **MAIL COUPON TODAY—NO-RISK 14 DAY FREE TRIAL** - - - - - - -

Simon & Schuster, Inc.
Simon & Schuster Building, 1230 Avenue of the Americas,
New York, N.Y. 10020, Mail Order Dept. 103

Please send me copies of the books checked above.
(If not completely satisfied, you may return for full refund within 14 days.)
☐ Save! Enclose full amount per *copy* with this coupon: publisher pays postage and handling: or charge my credit card.

☐ Master Card   ☐ Visa

My credit card number is_____

card expires_____

Signature_____

Name_____
                         (Please Print)
Address_____

City_____State_____Zip Code_____
or available at your local bookstore